B7j

SONGS
IN THE
NIGHT

DEVOTIONAL MESSAGES
FROM THE WORLDWIDE RADIO

WARREN W. WIERSBE

Baker Book House Grand Rapids, Michigan

Preface

The devotional messages in this book were originally given over "Songs in the Night," the international radio ministry of the Moody Memorial Church in Chicago, where I am privileged to serve as pastor. Because so many listeners wrote requesting copies of many of the messages, we thought it might be helpful to God's people if we compiled some of them in book form.

If our mail is any indication, "Songs in the Night" is ministering to a cross section of humanity: elderly retired people, university students, teen-agers, Christian workers, unbelievers, people who want to be believers, and just "plain people" with one kind of burden or another. Because our listening audience is so varied, the messages are varied; and this variety will be seen in the messages selected for this book. If some of these messages meet the needs in your life, I will be grateful to God.

I want to thank my secretary, Miss Marsha Maserang, for typing the manuscript from my edited scripts. Also, a word of appreciation to Don Smith, executive producer of "Songs in the Night," who encouraged me to put these messages together.

This year, "Songs in the Night" commemorates thirty years of broadcasting. Times have changed, and preachers have changed; but one thing has not changed: God still gives "songs in the night"!

Warren W. Wiersbe
The Moody Memorial Church
Chicago, Illinois

Contents

1

A Land of Hills and Valleys

For some reason, I have never enjoyed geography. Perhaps I didn't study hard enough in school. But as I study my Bible, I find myself becoming greatly interested in God's geography, particularly something that God said about the Promised Land He was giving to His people, Israel. "But the land you are going over to possess is a land of hills and valleys" (Deut. 11:11). I can't think of a better description of the Christian life—a land of hills and valleys.

Christians today have a great deal in common with the nation of Israel back in Moses' day, even though there are some radical differences. For example, there was a time when the people were in bondage; and God set them free. Once you and I were in bondage to sin; but God has set us free. God set Israel free by the blood of the lamb; and God has set us free by the blood of Jesus Christ, God's Lamb without spot or blemish. God led the nation with a cloud by day and a pillar of fire by night; and God leads us today through His Holy Word. God brought His people to the border of their inheritance and told them to go in and possess the land by faith; but, unfortunately, they fell into unbelief and failed to possess the land.

The Lord has given Christians today a wonderful spiritual inheritance in Christ, and all we have to do is possess it by faith. The Bible is the divine road map that describes our inheritance for us; and God says that our inheritance is "a land of hills and valleys."

Now, this fact may come as a surprise to some of you. Many people have the idea that the Christian life is an easy life—that once you are saved, your troubles are over. Well, once you are saved, many problems *are* solved; but many new problems appear. Jesus never promised that it would be easy for us to claim our inheritance. "In the world you will have tribulation," He warned His disciples. "If they have hated me, they will hate you." The Christian life is a land of hills and valleys.

Let's begin with the valleys. Have you ever noticed that most of the great people in the Bible went through valley experiences? In Genesis 15 I find Abraham going through "the horror of a great darkness." I find Isaac trembling because one of his sons has tricked him. I see Jacob wrestling all night until he is willing to surrender to God. I hear Moses crying out to God, "I am not able to bear all this people alone . . . kill me, I pray thee." I see David hiding in a cave and wondering if the crown would ever be on his head. I hear the prophet Isaiah lamenting, "I have labored in vain; I have spent my strength for nothing and in vain!" (Isa. 49:4). I watch John the Baptist in prison as he sends his disciples to Jesus to ask, "Are you the Messiah, or should we look for another?" Yes, I even hear the great apostle Paul saying, "For we would not have you ignorant, brethren, of our trouble which came to us in Asia, that we were pressed out of measure, above strength, insomuch that we despaired even of life." These men knew what it was to go through the valley.

Why does God permit these valleys to come to our lives? For one thing, we learn some lessons in the valleys that we could never learn on the mountaintop. Do you think that David could have written those wonderful psalms if he had never known the trials in the valley? How could he have written, "Yea, though I walk through the valley of the

8

shadow of death, I will fear no evil, for thou art with me," if he had never gone through the valley himself? Suppose Jeremiah had never gone through that terrible valley that made him the "Weeping Prophet"? Could he ever have written, "His compassions fail not; they are new every morning; great is thy faithfulness" (Lam. 3:22, 23)? Suppose Paul had never gone through the valley with his thorn in the flesh? Could he have written, "My grace is sufficient for thee"? When we go through the valley, we learn lessons we could never learn any other way.

And, we grow in character in a way that we could never grow apart from the valley. Great Christians are made by great trials. A man does not become patient simply by reading a book or praying a prayer. He becomes patient by going through the valley. We don't learn how to pray by sitting in an easy chair. We learn how to pray by going through the valley. Faith is cultivated in the darkness of the valley. God may *teach* us in the light, but He *tests* us in the darkness. This is why Paul wrote: "But we had the sentence of death in ourselves, that we should not trust in ourselves, but in God which raiseth the dead." The Christian graces are developed as we walk with Christ through the valley.

But God has another purpose for the valley: as we go through the valley, we learn how to help others. Psalm 84:6 puts it this way: "Who passing through the valley of weeping makes it a place of springs." Here is a pilgrim going through a difficult valley, so difficult he is even weeping; but he leaves behind a well to refresh the pilgrims that will follow him. Perhaps the reason you are in the valley today is that God may comfort you so you in turn may comfort someone else. He wants you to leave a well behind. Paul had this in mind when he wrote, "God comforts us in all our tribulation that we may be able to comfort them which are in any trouble, by the comfort wherewith we ourselves are comforted of God" (II Cor. 1:4).

The Christian life is a land of hills and valleys. God ordains the valleys that He might teach us lessons we could never learn any other way. He leads us through the valleys so that

9

we may grow in our Christian character, and so that we may help others when they go through the valley. But there's a fourth reason He permits the valleys, and it's this: you cannot have hills unless you have valleys.

Wouldn't it be wonderful if life were just a series of mountaintop experiences? Wouldn't we be happier if there were no valleys in our lives? The Christian life is a land of hills and valleys, but we must never forget that you cannot have hills unless you have valleys.

God knows how to balance our lives. All sunshine makes a desert, says the old proverb; and all hills, without valleys, will make an immature and shallow life. If you and I want to enjoy the hilltops of happiness, we must be willing to experience the valleys of trial. It's comforting and encouraging to know that at the end of every valley there is a hill, and atop that hill is a new experience of blessing from the Lord.

I can't help but notice that the lives of God's people in the Bible were made up of both hills and valleys. Abraham received a great promise from God one day, and the next day the land was plunged into drought and famine. Isaac was born, and Abraham's joy was complete. A few years later, God told him to offer his beloved son on the altar. The great prophet Moses experienced his hills and valleys. No sooner had he led the nation out of Egypt when they began to complain and ask to go back into bondage! Moses met God on the mountaintop and saw His glory; then he came down and discovered Israel dancing before a golden idol. Hills and valleys!

It was true even in the earthly life of our Lord. When Jesus was baptized in the Jordan River, the Father spoke from heaven and the Spirit came down on Jesus like a dove. What a mountaintop experience! But then the Spirit drove Jesus into the wilderness to be tempted by the devil. What a valley to go through! See Him as He enters Gethsemane, as He prays and sweats great drops of blood. See Him hanging on a cross! What a valley He endured! But then, see Him risen from the dead—radiant in the glorified body! What a mountaintop experience! Then He ascends to the highest heaven and sits at the right hand of God!

This is God's word of encouragement to you as you go through the valley. He has a glorious blessing waiting for you at the end of the valley. The Christian life is a land of hills and valleys; and wherever you find a valley, you will always find a mountaintop at the other end. This is true because our Lord Jesus Christ has already gone before us to prepare the way. Every valley that we go through, Christ has already traveled before us.

I'm glad the Christian life is a land of hills and valleys. There is nothing monotonous about it. Every day presents a new challenge to grow in grace, a new opportunity to help others, a new privilege to receive grace and strength from Jesus Christ. It is a land of hills and valleys, and our God is a God of the hills and a God of the valleys.

2

It Takes Time to Make Things Beautiful

It's good to know that the word *beautiful* has returned to our vocabulary. We're accustomed now to hearing people talk about beautiful ideas, beautiful thoughts, and even beautiful people. As I thought about this recently, I recalled a verse from the Bible: "He hath made everything beautiful in his time" (Eccles. 3:11). To me, this is a very encouraging statement; and I want to explore it with you. "God hath made everything beautiful in His time."

This statement does not say that God has made everything beautiful, because He hasn't. Sin certainly isn't beautiful, but God did not make sin. Hatred is not beautiful, but God is not the author of hatred. God is love. Violence is not beautiful, but God did not create violence. Violence is borne out of the selfish hearts of men, not out of the loving heart of God. Whether we like it or not, there are some things in this life that are not beautiful; but these are the things men have made, not God.

No, our verse tells us that all the things that God has made have their own beauty in their own time; and that's quite a different story. You can see this principle at work in nature. In the winter season, the landscape is barren and dreary. If a visitor from outer space were to arrive in Chicago during the heart of winter, he might wonder why people enjoy living there! There are times when Mother Nature wears garments of mourning; at those times there isn't a great deal of beauty to admire.

But then the spring arrives, and everything begins to change! Those ugly stumps in the garden start to develop into roses. The trees sprout their leaves and the grass begins to turn green. And before long, you and I forget the dark, cold winter and commence to enjoy the beauty of springtime. "God hath made everything beautiful *in his time.*"

To some degree, I think this is true in human life as well. A newborn baby can hardly be called beautiful! Of course we love the baby and look beyond its initial features, but you really don't expect a newborn baby to be beautiful. But time takes care of the matter; and before long you have a darling child, then a lovely teen-ager, and then a truly beautiful adult. "God hath made everything beautiful *in his time.*"

Now, this statement from the Bible tells us two important facts. First, that God's desire is for beauty; God is not interested in ugliness. Second, that you and I need patience to wait for God to bring the beauty in His own time. Of course when we talk about beauty, we do not mean the artificial glamour that the world admires. We mean the true inner beauty that reveals itself in gracious character and conduct. God's will for our lives is that we share in true beauty and if we wait for Him to work, He will bring that beauty in His own time. Artificial beauty is always available, but true beauty from God can come only in God's time.

Let's apply this principle to our lives personally. God wants our lives to be beautiful, because God is glorified by beautiful things. But this beauty is not something that comes automatically; it is the result of the difficult process of living. True beauty of character can never be purchased at a cosmetic counter; it must come from the heart. Of course, the first step toward this beauty is receiving Christ into the heart as Savior. He must cleanse us from the ugliness of sin and fill us with the beauty of holiness before our lives can truly begin to take on that Christ-likeness that we need.

After we have turned our lives over to Christ, we must yield to His will and let Him make us the way He wants us to be. This often means going through times of testing and trial. Perhaps today you are going through the furnace of suffering, and you may be asking, "Why is this happening to me?" As you look at your situation, you don't see much beauty; but remember, God makes everything beautiful *in His time.* I have been through times of suffering and certainly didn't see much beauty in them; but after a few years, God's purposes were fulfilled and the true beauty of the experience was revealed.

I think of that young man Joseph in the Book of Genesis—sold as a slave by his brothers, forced to do a servant's work in Egypt, thrown into prison because of a vicious lie. It seems such an ugly picture! But God was at work, and ultimately the beauty of the whole picture was revealed. Then Joseph was able to say to this brothers, "You meant it to me for evil, but God meant it for good." God made Joseph's experiences beautiful in their time.

I think of Stephen, the first Christian martyr. His enemies lied about him and brought false witnesses into court. As Stephen tried to tell them about Christ, they dragged him out of the city and stoned him to death. What an ugly scene—that hateful mob throwing stones at an innocent man. But God made it beautiful in His time; for as the result of Stephen's shining face, Saul of Tarsus was saved and became the great apostle Paul.

If you are in the will of God, no matter how dark your situation may be, remember this: God has a plan, God has a time, and God will make everything beautiful in His time.

This principle is seen at work especially in the life of Jesus Christ. You will remember that the prophet Isaiah had this to say about Jesus: "For he shall grow up before him as a tender plant, and as a root out of a dry ground: he hath no form nor comeliness, and when we shall see him, there is no beauty that we should desire him" (Isa. 53:2).

From a purely human point of view, there was nothing beautiful about Jesus Christ. Certainly *His birth* was not beautiful: He was born in a cattle stall surrounded by poverty. He grew up in a poor carpenter's home in Nazareth, and there was a proverb in that day which said, "Can any good thing come out of Nazareth?" "Despised and rejected of men"—"There is no beauty that we should desire him."

During His ministry He was known as the friend of sinners. The lowest sinner could come up to Jesus and talk to Him. Most of the important people steered clear of Jesus; they didn't like the company He kept.

How did He die? The worst possible death—crucifixion. There was nothing beautiful in His death; it was ugly, violent, painful, and shameful. "He hath no form nor comeliness . . . there is no beauty that we should desire him."

But, remember—God has made everything beautiful *in His time.* When you trust Christ as your Savior, then you look at Him with spiritual perception and you see His beauty. You see the beauty of His birth. Paul puts it this way: "For you know the grace of our Lord Jesus Christ, that though he was rich, yet for your sakes he became poor, that you through his poverty might be rich" (II Cor. 8:9). And we see the beauty of *His life*—the good shepherd seeking the lost sheep, the great physician seeking to heal the wounds of humanity. Yes, we even see the beauty of *His death.* Paul wrote, "God forbid that I should glory save in the cross of our Lord Jesus Christ" (Gal. 6:14). In fact, we Christians remember Christ's death every time we observe the Lord's Supper.

The beauty of Jesus Christ captivates the person who trusts Him and lives for Him. We long to be conformed to the image of Christ! The psalmist looked at Jesus Christ through the telescope of faith and wrote, "Thou art fairer than the children of men; grace is poured into thy lips" (45:2). The one who believes on Christ sees how beautiful the Savior is and longs to become just like Him.

"God hath made everything beautiful in his time." Wait on

the Lord, let Him work out His plan, and one day you will see the beauty of it all. Meanwhile, lose yourself in the beauty of Jesus Christ. Let God transform you to become more like Christ! And one day, that beauty will be revealed in glory when Jesus returns for His own.

3

Is Your Watchdog Awake?

A lady in Texas purchased a watchdog to protect her property. After a few days, she discovered that the dog was prone to go to sleep. Instead of trading in the dog for a more alert animal, she did an unusual thing. She purchased a duck; and whenever the duck saw the dog dozing, the duck would begin to quack and peck at him! Whether or not this solved the problem, I don't know; but reading that news item started me thinking: I wonder if *my* watchdog is awake?

Every man needs a watchdog, not to protect his material possessions, but to protect something far more valuable: his moral and spiritual possessions. If someone steals your camera, you can always buy another one; but if someone steals your honesty or your integrity, you will have a difficult time replacing them. The treasures on the inside are far more valuable than those on the outside; so every man must take care to guard his character.

Of course, there are many people who scoff at such an idea. They say, "What difference does it make if I lose my character, just so long as I am a success in the world?" Well, it depends on what you mean by "a success." If a man is a winner financially but a loser morally, you can hardly call him a success. What a man *is* certainly is far more important than what a man *has*. When someone asked financial wizard J. P. Morgan what the best bank collateral was, Morgan replied, "A man's character."

Many people live for reputation; and, of course, a good reputation is desirable. But reputation is only what people *think* we are; character is what God *knows* we are. This is why D. L. Moody once said, "If I take care of my character, my reputation will take care of itself."

No, having a good reputation before men is not quite the same as cultivating a true character before God. Many people enjoy a good reputation, not because they are known, but because they are *unknown:* nobody really knows the secrets of their hearts. As one writer has put it, "Many a man's *reputation* would not know his *character* if they met on the street." Next to trusting Christ as Savior, the most important thing in life is building a true character before God and men.

Now, to help us build this character, God has given us a watchdog. It is called conscience. Conscience is that inner judge that warns us when we have done wrong, or praises us when we have done right. Conscience is the voice of God in the soul of a person. Conscience is the moral watchdog that warns us when a thief is approaching. When a person is making a decision, he hears several voices from his inner being. Cowardice asks, "Is it safe?" Greed asks, "Is it profitable?" Vanity asks, "Is it popular?" But conscience asks, "Is it right?"

Jesus must have had conscience in mind when He said, "The light of the body is the eye: if therefore thine eye be single, thy whole body shall be full of light. But if thine eye be evil, thy whole body shall be full of darkness. If therefore the light that is in thee be darkness, how great is that darkness!" (Matt. 6:22-23). How important it is to have a conscience that is strong and healthy—a watchdog that is awake.

Like a delicate scientific instrument, conscience can be damaged. In fact, a man's conscience can be so damaged that he would call light darkness and darkness light! There is even a conscience among thieves, so that if one betrays another, he feels remorse. Conscience is like a window that lets in the light of God's truth. If the window is allowed to get dirty, then less and less light comes in; and the person feels less and less judgment when he disobeys God.

It was an American Indian who illustrated conscience to one of the former pastors of the Moody Church, Dr. Harry Ironside. The Indian said: "It is like an arrowhead in my heart. If I do something wrong, the arrowhead turns and cuts me. But, if I keep on doing wrong, the corners are finally worn down, and the arrowhead doesn't cut me anymore." Or, to use our original comparison, the watchdog goes to sleep.

The Bible tells us that there is more than one kind of conscience. There is a *good* conscience, for example. "And herein do I exercise myself, to have always a conscience void of offense toward God and toward men" (Acts 24:16). A good conscience is one that is exercised—it isn't allowed to go to sleep. When it speaks, we listen and obey.

But there is also a *defiled* conscience. "Unto the pure all things are pure: but unto them that are defiled and unbelievers, nothing is pure; but even their mind and conscience is defiled" (Titus 1:15). The man with a defiled conscience finds dirty things in a clean conversation. He can practice what he calls "little sins" and still go to sleep at night. A defiled conscience is the result of repeated sin—sin that is loved and cultivated secretly. If you and I are permitting something in our lives that a year ago would have kept us awake, then conscience is defiled.

The Bible also talks about a *"seared* conscience." "Speaking lies in hypocrisy, having their conscience seared with a hot iron" (I Tim. 4:2). If you have ever been burned, you know what this is all about. Nature covers a burn with a hard layer of skin to protect the sensitive place, and you lose your feeling in the area. The word *seared* in this verse is actually our medical word *cauterize.* A defiled conscience ultimately becomes a seared conscience, and all feeling is gone.

When that happens, the watchdog is dead—the light becomes darkness—the judge is no longer on the bench—the sharp arrowhead has lost its cutting edge—the delicate compass no longer points true north. When this happens, a man's character has deteriorated; and it won't be long before everybody knows it. "If the light that is in thee be darkness," said Jesus, "how great is that darkness!"

A man is not saved by character, he is saved by faith in Jesus Christ. The lowest sinner and highest moral man both stand guilty before God, and both need a Savior. "For there is no difference, for all have sinned and come short of the glory of God" (Rom. 3:22-23). Because of Christ's death on the cross, it is possible for a man to have his conscience cleansed and put back in working order again. God's grace can radically change a man. "If any man be in Christ he is a new creature; old things are passed away, behold, all things are become new" (II Cor. 5:17).

When a man's character is decaying, he lives in constant fear that other people will discover his secrets. For months, perhaps for years, he will sin against his conscience and eventually put the watchdog to sleep. Secret sin takes its toll in his life. Is there any hope for this man?

Yes, there is! Jesus Christ can take that life and give that man a new beginning. I am not saying that he will not reap what he has sown; but I am saying that Jesus Christ can forgive him and cleanse his conscience. "Let us draw near with a true heart in full assurance of faith, having our hearts sprinkled from an evil conscience" (Heb. 10:22). The blood of Jesus Christ can cleanse the heart and the conscience, making that man a child of God.

There are two conditions that must be met. The first is *truth:* "Let us draw near with a true heart." We can deceive ourselves and even deceive others, but we cannot deceive God. The time comes for us to be open and honest with God and with ourselves and to admit sin. This is the moment of truth. We come to God and say, "I am going to hide and pretend no longer. Search me, O God, and know my heart!"

The second condition is *faith:* "Let us draw near with a

20

true heart in full assurance of faith." A man is saved and cleansed, not by works, but by faith. Faith means surrendering to God on His terms. It means yielding to Jesus Christ and asking Him to save you. "He that believeth on him [Christ] is not condemned, but he that believeth not is condemned already" (John 3:18). "For by grace are ye saved through faith" (Eph. 2:8).

When Jesus Christ comes into the life, He makes the sinner into a new person. He puts His life in the heart. He cleanses the defiled conscience and causes it to function as it should, so that we can start to build a true Christian character. This means no more deception—no more fear of getting caught—no more agony trying to live a double life.

A good conscience is a priceless treasure, because a good conscience means a godly character. Don't let the watchdog go to sleep! With the apostle Paul, strive to maintain a conscience void of offense toward men and toward God.

4

The Secret of Encouragement

All of us have our crisis days when everything seems to fall apart, days when it looks as if we have come to the end of the road and that God has turned against us. In I Samuel 30 we see David experiencing such a crisis. He had just returned from battle to discover that the enemy had attacked his camp, taken all his goods, and, worse yet, kidnapped all the wives and children. So serious was the situation that his own men talked about stoning him. How did David face this crisis? Listen to what the Bible says: "But David encouraged himself in the Lord his God."

A crisis does not *make* a man; a crisis *reveals* what the man is made of. Character is not built in the crisis experiences of life. Character is built in the day-by-day experiences, the little decisions and actions that never attract attention. But what we really are is revealed for everyone to see when a crisis comes our way.

It's interesting to see how David's men reacted when they discovered their terrible loss. Some sat and wept until they had no more tears to shed. Others complained and blamed David, and some even suggested that they stone their leader.

You wonder how that would have solved the problem; yet people do the same thing today. How easy it is in a crisis to blame somebody else, or to look for a scapegoat. But what did David do? Well, he shed tears like the rest of the soldiers because he, too, loved his family. But after that, he stopped feeling sorry for himself and he turned to the Lord for help. "But David encouraged himself in the Lord his God."

How can you and I today get the encouragement we need in the crisis hours of life? Certainly the Lord is able to carry us through. Nothing is impossible with God. There is no problem of life too difficult for Him to solve. What, then, should we do in order to receive God's gracious encouragement? Let me suggest some simple steps to take—in fact, the very steps that David took.

First, surrender to the will of the Lord. David asked the priest to bring him the ephod, which was that special priestly device for determining the will of God. David asked the Lord if he should pursue after the enemy, and God told him "Yes." Then David asked if he and his men would recover their loved ones and their possessions, and again God said, "Yes." So, before David made any move, he first determined the will of God in the matter.

You see, my friend, there are no accidents, only appointments. The crisis hours of life don't come as a surprise to God. He knows the end from the beginning, and He knew long ago that you would need His help today. When a crisis hour invades our lives, the first thing we should do is surrender to the will of the Lord. God has a purpose of fulfill; and if we surrender to Him, it will all work out for our good and His glory. To fight God's will, complain, and blame others is but to miss the blessing God has for us in these experiences. David encouraged himself in the Lord his God by surrendering to God's will.

But David didn't stop there. The next thing he did was to ask God for the strength to do what needed to be done. David and his men were tired from battle, and the emotional strain of the crisis had weakened them. But in obedience to the Lord, they mounted and rode off in pursuit of the

23

enemy. Where did David and his men get the strength they needed? God gave it to them. When God tells us to do something, He always gives us the strength we need to obey.

Now, David and his men could have argued with God. They could have said, "Lord, we just came back from the war. We're tired and hungry. And our hearts are broken because our dear ones have been kidnapped. Can't we spend the night here and get some rest?" But they didn't say that. David commanded them to secure their weapons. They mounted their animals, and off they went to conquer the enemy. God gave them the strength they needed, and God will give you the strength you need in your hour of crisis.

It's wonderful the way God has equipped the human body for crisis experiences. When a crisis arises, our glands begin to pour out extra energy into the bloodstream; and it's amazing what we can do when we really have to do it. No man is so brave or so strong as the man who sees his loved ones in danger and goes to rescue them. In a similar way, God has equipped us to have extra spiritual strength just when we need it. The Christian who walks with God, who prays and reads God's Word, discovers unusual strength from the Lord in the crisis hours of life.

David depended on God's strength, not his own. You and I can never make it through the crises if we lean on our own power. That promise in Isaiah 40:31 is so practical: "They that wait upon the Lord shall renew their strength; they shall mount up with wings as eagles; they shall run and not be weary, they shall walk and not faint."

The wonderful thing about being a Christian is that we have a strength not our own. Paul wrote, "I can do all things through Christ who strengtheneth me" (Phil. 4:13). I like the way J. B. Phillips translates this verse: "I am ready for anything through the strength of the one who lives within me." This is the second step in facing the crisis hour. First, we surrender to God's will; then, we depend on God's strength. And the strength of the Lord never fails.

But there is a third step: David trusted God to do the rest. How would David ever find where his enemies were hiding? And if he did find them, suppose they were stronger than his army? Was there enough time left? Perhaps the enemy had already killed the wives and little children? So many questions went through David's mind, but then he just turned it all over to the Lord and trusted God to work.

God did work in a wonderful way, for He led David right to the enemy camp. They caught the enemy by surprise and recovered all of their wealth and their loved ones, plus the loot the enemy left behind! It was a great victory; and, like all spiritual victories, it was a victory of faith. "And this is the victory that overcomes . . . even our faith."

Four times in the Bible we read, "The just shall live by faith." We are saved by faith, but that's only the beginning: we are supposed to *live* by faith. When the crisis hours break upon us, there are some things we can do, but there are many things we cannot do. And this is where faith comes in. "Commit thy way unto the Lord, trust also in him, and he shall bring it to pass" (Ps. 37:5). Like David, we must do what God tells us to do. But, also like David, we must trust God to do those things that we cannot do ourselves.

Faith is a practical thing; it controls the actions of our lives. The way we believe determines how we behave. David set out in pursuit of the enemy, trusting that God would direct him and give him the victory; and God honored his faith. When the child of God is doing the will of God, he can expect the hand of God to work for him.

Right now, you may not see how your particular problem is going to be solved; but God sees, and that's all that matters. If you look at yourself, you'll get discouraged. If you look at the circumstances around you, you'll get discouraged. But if by faith you look to Jesus Christ, then, like David, you will "encourage yourself in the Lord your God." As you read His Word and rest on His promises, your faith will grow and God will lead you a step at a time out of your crisis and into His victory.

In these difficult days, learn the secret of encouraging yourself in the Lord your God. Surrender to God's will, depend on God's strength, and rest on God's promises by faith. As you do, your discouragement will eventually fade and God will give you wonderful victory.

5

Salt of the Earth

You have had the experience, I'm sure. Your dinner is set before you and you take that first delicious bite—only to discover that the cook left out the salt. Or perhaps you have been a patient in the hospital and the doctor ordered a salt-free diet. Salt is such a little thing—such a common thing—that we take it for granted. But how big it becomes when it isn't there! Jesus looked at His disciples one day and said, "Ye are the salt of the earth." What did Jesus mean when He made that statement?

There are two substances mentioned in the Bible that are small but very important: salt and yeast, or leaven. They picture opposite forces in our world. Salt is antiseptic; it holds back decay. Yeast is actually a mold, and in the Bible it represents evil. The Old Testament Jews were instructed not to put yeast in their sacrifices because yeast symbolized sin. But they were instructed to add salt to their sacrifices. Salt pictured holiness, the power of righteousness to hold back decay.

Jesus calls His disciples "the salt of the earth." In other words, Christians are to the world what salt is to food. People in Bible times didn't have refrigeration as we do today; so they seasoned their meat with salt to keep it from decaying. Jesus sees today's world as a rotting mass of sin, and He has put Christians into this world to help hold back the decay. We are the salt of the earth.

Did you ever stop to consider what society would be like if there were no Christians? The church of Jesus Christ for two thousand years has been spreading righteousness and holding back sin. It was because of Christians spreading the gospel that women and children were freed from bondage. It was the message of preachers of the gospel like John Wesley and George Whitefield that saved England from revolution and ruin. Child labor laws, poor laws, the abolition of slavery, educational opportunities—all of these are a direct result of the witness of the church. Hospitals, orphanages, homes for the aged, care for the underprivileged—these, too, are the fruit of the gospel.

Now we must confess that the church has not done all it could do! But we thank God that some of the salt has penetrated society to help people who are in need. After all, that's why Jesus left us here in this world. In John 17, Jesus said, "I pray not that thou shouldest take them out of the world." Jesus actually prayed that we would stay in the world and have an influence for good. We are the salt of the earth; and if salt is functioning as it should, it helps to hold back corruption.

Never underestimate the influence of even one Christian. You may feel that your life is not accomplishing very much; but if you are faithful to the Lord, He is using you as salt to accomplish His will where you are. I want to warn you, however, that when salt is applied, it often stings. Those around us don't always appreciate the presence of the salt. They feel more at home with the yeast. So, if others seem to shun you or resent you, don't be discouraged. This may mean that the salt is having its proper effect.

Salt not only holds back decay, it also seasons and makes food more palatable. That's an exciting thought: we Christians are God's seasoning in the world! We are here to help make life more enjoyable for others. Unfortunately, some people are not seasoning—they are poison! They make life bitter and difficult. I suppose all of us can think of some people we know who are always complaining, always grumbling; and they make life miserable for themselves and for others. I have a pastor friend who told me that he has one prayer that he prays constantly: "Lord, help me not to add to anyone's burdens." That's a good prayer to pray!

Crystals of salt are tiny, but what a difference they make in the taste of an egg. We Christians may not seem very large and imposing, but what a difference we can make in an office or a neighborhood. I think of the apostle Paul on board that ship going to Rome. You remember how the storm came and nobody knew what to do. Well, Paul took the helm of that ship and told them what God wanted them to do; and he saved the lives of 276 men. He encouraged them when the nights were the darkest. He was God's salt on board that ship.

I think of Joseph back in the Old Testament, serving in the land of Egypt. He was God's salt. Even when he was put into prison, he still flavored the prison and brought encouragement and help. What a wonderful way to live—being God's salt to season life and help others. There are some experiences of life that really don't "taste" too good, and the addition of a little salt—some Christian kindness—can make such a difference.

A few years ago, a speeding driver hit my car and almost took my life. It was a trying experience for my wife and family. But no sooner did she reach the hospital after the accident than our Christian friends began to arrive to stand with her. My accident was a difficult experience, but our friends added the salt that helped to make it sweeter.

We are the salt of the earth. As salt, we are helping to hold back the growth of corruption in this world; and as salt, we are seasoning life to make it more enjoyable for others. The important thing is that we don't allow the world to rob us of our flavor. Jesus said, "If the salt loses its saltiness, how can it be salted again?" We must maintain that close walk with

God that keeps us at our best. Only then can we effectively minister as the salt of the earth.

But salt has another use: salt makes people thirsty. I received a letter from the husband of one of our church members, asking me not to visit him or try to influence him to attend church. He didn't want the pastor to call on him, nor did he want any of the men to call on him. I wrote and told him I would honor his request, and that I would pray for him. A year later that man showed up in church, and at the closing hymn he came forward to dedicate his life and come back into fellowship with the church family.

Do you know what it was that brought him back? He told me what it was—the godly life of his devoted Christian wife. She didn't preach any sermons. She didn't nag him or argue with him. She just prayed for him and lived before him a life that glorified God. She was the salt in that home, and her life made that husband thirsty for what she had.

I recall another man who attended church faithfully but had never made any profession of faith in Christ. Then one Sunday he boldly came down the aisle, professed his faith, and asked to be received into the membership of the church. I asked him, "What influenced you to make this important decision?" He said nothing about my sermon or the music or even the visits of the church family. He pointed to a young couple in the congretation, a couple who had recently gone through a very trying experience. He said, "Pastor, I've watched them; and I've seen how they have acted during this difficult time. And I said to myself, 'I need what they have.'" You see, my friend, that couple was salt in his life—they made him thirsty for the blessings of the Christian life.

You are familiar, I'm sure, with Paul's experience in that Philippian jail, recorded in Acts 16. Did you ever ask yourself what it was that made the jailer want to be saved? It wasn't the earthquake—that almost drove him to suicide. It was Paul's attitude that touched the man. "Do thyself no harm," Paul shouted, "for we are all here." After the way Paul had been treated by the jailer, you would think he would want to see the man punished. No, Paul practiced being salt; and when Paul returned love for hatred, he saw the man awakened and brought to Christ.

Salt holds back decay, salt gives flavor to life, and salt makes people thirsty. And Jesus says of you and me, "Ye are the salt of the earth."

6

Avoiding the Accidents of Life

The National Safety Council is greatly concerned about the slaughter on the highways. Each year thousands of people are killed, and millions more are maimed and injured because of auto accidents. You'll be interested to know that studies have revealed two basic causes for most of the serious accidents: excessive speed and failure to yield the right-of-way. When I read that news item, I thought to myself, "Those are the very causes of the *human* collisions and tragedies of life: people exceed the spiritual speed limit and rush ahead of God's will, or else they fail to yield the right-of-way to God." No wonder David wrote in Psalm 32:9, "Be not as the horse or as the mule . . . ," because those two animals illustrate the cause of trouble in our lives.

Some people are like the horse: they can't wait—they have to rush ahead even when they aren't sure where they are going. And some people are like the mule: they hold back and simply won't yield their will to anybody. These are the basic causes of accidents on our highways—exceeding the speed limit and failing to yield the right-of-way—and they also cause accidents in our everyday lives.

I have a friend who is constantly rushing into things without taking time to think, pray, and seek God's will. He's like the horse—he's impulsive. I'm sure all of us have made impulsive decisions at one time or another, and we've lived to regret them. But my friend makes it a habit to plunge into new ventures without carefully considering what lies ahead. Consequently, he is forever trying to rescue himself from embarrassing and costly mistakes. Because he runs ahead of God's will, he misses God's blessing.

I will never forget a lesson I learned from a godly professor when I was attending seminary. Some of us were preaching each weekend and really enjoying it, so much so that some of the men thought they would drop out of school and devote their full time to the ministry. After all, they argued, it's more important to work for God than to earn a degree. One of the professors solved the problem with a single statement. He quietly said, "Men, the Lord has been waiting a long time for you to come along; and I'm sure He can wait another year."

That professor was right: God is never frantically in a hurry. You will never find Jesus Christ rushing into situations. When God is at work He works with calmness and precision, not with haste and carelessness. In fact, there are several men in the Bible who became impulsive and ran ahead of God; and they paid dearly for their mistakes. Moses rushed ahead of God's will and killed that Egyptian, and it cost him forty years of waiting in the wilderness. Peter rushed ahead of God's will and cut off a man's ear; and had Jesus not healed the man, it would have cost Peter his life. Abraham ran ahead of God and married Hagar, and their son Ishmael brought trouble to their home.

"Be not as the horse"—don't exceed the speed limit, don't run ahead of God. One of the marks of maturity is patience, a willingness to wait for God's time. God is never too early, God is never too late. Obey His will and your timing will never be wrong. But it is also important that we not lag behind. We must not be guilty of stubbornly failing to yield the right-of-way, like the mule. If you have done any driving at all on our big city expressways, you know how important it is to yield the right-of-way. Not to yield will inevitably mean a collision. This is why you see that triangular sign at every point of entry: "Yield right-of-way."

God asks us to yield to Him. He knows far better than we do what is best for our lives; and, as we have often heard, "God always gives His best to those who leave the choice with Him." The driver who speeds onto the expressway without watching the traffic is only committing suicide; and, sad to say, he may take the lives of innocent people. But this is true in the spiritual realm as well: if I fail to yield to God, it will hurt me and it will also hurt others.

Yielding the right-of-way is the secret of success in our homes. After I perform a marriage, I usually say to the couple: "Now, remember, it's no longer *yours* or *mine:* it's *ours.*" The husband who decides to do what he wants to do, regardless of what his wife wants, is heading for a collision. The wife who intends to continue her independence even after marriage is asking for an accident. A happy home is the result of two people willing to yield the right-of-way, first to the Lord and then to each other.

This is the secret of a successful church. Church members who insist on having their own way (or else they'll resign from the board or leave the church) are helping to cause tragic accidents, and the result could be the breaking up of a testimony for God. Paul had this in mind when he wrote to the Philippians, "Let nothing be done through strife or vain glory, but in lowliness of mind, let each esteem others more important than themselves" (2:3). Have you ever noticed in the four Gospels how often the disciples argued over who was the greatest? Jesus tried to teach them that the humble person, the one who stoops to serve others, was the greatest.

The Christian who fails to yield the right-of-way wants to have his own way, and the person who lives like this is dangerous to have around. He may call his attitude "conviction," but God would call it "stubbornness." He may be proud of the fact that he will not give in, but God is grieved because the man will not yield the right-of-way. And the man who fails to yield the right-of-way to God fails to receive the blessings God has for him.

One of the wonderful things about the Christian life is the fact that we are a part of a great plan. God has a perfect plan for our lives and He reveals this plan to us a step at a time. Living the Christian life is not like building a hi-fi set. God doesn't give you all the pieces at one time, with a complete blueprint to follow. No, He reveals His will to us a step at a time; and He supplies the necessary parts as we need them.

The first step in realizing and enjoying God's plan is simply yielding to His will. We must take our own hands off and let His hands hold us and direct us. This means that we don't tell God what to do; He tells us what to do. This involves reading His Word, the Bible, because in the Bible God reveals His will. This also means spending time in sincere prayer, because as we pray, God works in us by His Holy Spirit; and the Holy Spirit gives us guidance. Yielding to God is a day-by-day experience. It isn't a decision we make once in a church service, and then forget about it. No, we must yield to Him anew each day that we live.

As God reveals His will to us, we must be willing to do it. Jesus said, "If any man is willing to do his will, he shall know of the doctrine" (John 7:17). God reveals His will to the willing heart, not to the curious or frivolous. If we become like the mule, and refuse to yield, then God has to discipline us.

There are times in our lives when we really don't know what to do. I'm sure you have had experiences like this. You have a decision to make; you have prayed about it and searched the Word, but you aren't sure what steps to take. What should you do? The answer, my friend, is this: *wait on the Lord*. Don't make an impulsive decision—don't exceed God's speed limit. Your times are in His hands. God is the one who winds the clock of life, and His timing is never off. The psalmist wrote, "Wait on the Lord," and the writer of Hebrews said, "But you have need of patience that after having done the will of God you might receive the promises" (10:36).

34

I trust that none of us will experience any accidents on the road of life. If we do, it will be the result of our own mistakes—either failing to yield the right-of-way or exceeding God's speed limit. God's timing is never wrong. If you don't know His will, then wait on the Lord. If you do know His will, then step out by faith and obey it. Be not as the horse or the mule; rather, be as the obedient sheep that follows the Good Shepherd.

7

A Gift of Peace and Rest

He stood in the busy marketplace in Capernaum, and everybody knew who He was. He was Jesus of Nazareth, the teacher, the healer. And He looked at the crowds as they rushed here and there, just the way the crowds rush at State and Madison in Chicago or Fifth and Vine in Cincinnati, or 42nd and Broadway in New York City . . . and this is what Jesus said: "Come unto me all ye that labor and are heavy laden, and I will give you rest." Rest! The thing millions of people are searching for today.

You can go to any drug store and purchase sleep, but you cannot purchase rest. Rest is not a condition of the body, it is a condition of the spirit—the inner man. I recall a patient saying to me in the hospital one day, "I slept last night, but I didn't rest. I woke up as tired as I was when I went to sleep."

Over a century ago, Henry David Thoreau looked at the busy people of his day, and wrote in his journal: "The mass of men lead lives of quiet desperation." One afternoon I visited Thoreau's hideaway at Walden Pond, and he should see it today! Super highways surround the unruffled pond; and thousands of vehicles pass it daily, polluting the air and disturbing the quiet atmosphere. There is a restlessness in the hearts of people today, and this restlessness reveals itself in many different ways.

Think, for example, of the health problems we face. Doctors tell us that half of the people in our hospital beds are not physically sick at all. People complain of headaches, backaches, neck problems, fatigue, and a host of other problems; and yet the doctors often can find nothing physically wrong with the patient. More than once a medical doctor has phoned me and said, "Pastor, I have a patient who needs spiritual help. Can you see him? I can give him medicine, but it would only relieve the symptoms. He needs God's help to remove the causes."

Think, too, of the social problems we face because of this inner restlessness. Husbands and wives cannot get along with each other. Children rebel against their parents. And one of the reasons there is war on the outside is simply because there is war on the inside. When a man is not at peace with God and with himself, he can never be at peace with his fellow men.

The tragedy is that people fail to recognize this inner restlessness; so they blame their unhappiness on everything else or everybody else. Then they try to find peace in "going places and doing things." They start to live on substitutes, and substitutes can never give a man peace. You can buy entertainment, but you cannot buy real joy. You can purchase pleasure, but nobody can sell you inner satisfaction. There is only one way to secure peace in your heart, and that is by receiving it from Jesus Christ. Peace is not a goal that we achieve, it is a gift that we receive. Jesus said, "I will give you rest."

The root cause of man's restlessness is sin. Long ago, the prophet Isaiah diagnosed the sickness of society when he wrote, "There is no peace, saith my Lord, to the wicked. The wicked are like the troubled sea" (57:20-21).

What is there about sin that takes away a man's peace? Well, to begin with, sin is basically rebellion against God; and when you declare war on God, you can never have peace.

37

When a man lives by faith in Christ, then everything in the universe works for him. But when he declares war on God, everything starts working against him.

Something else is true: sin makes us feel guilty. God made us that way. He put into our very personality a judge called "conscience," and this judge cries "Guilty!" every time we disobey God's law. Of course, it's possible to strangle the conscience, or even train it to approve what is evil; but even then, something deep inside keeps accusing us and robbing us of our peace.

Sin causes restlessness because sin is not a part of God's plan for our lives. Sin is an intruder. God made man to worship and serve Him, to enjoy and glorify Him; but sin makes a man worship himself and glorify himself. And when a man becomes self-centered, he loses that peace that comes only when God is controlling his life. To be sure, there is pleasure in sin for a season; but before long, we start reaping what we have sown.

I think another reason why sin makes people restless is the fact that sin makes us feel lonely. Sin cuts us off from God's fellowship, and when we lose that contact with God we feel lonely down inside. This explains why we have a difficult time sinning alone, and why we always have to tell somebody about it or, worse yet, get somebody else involved in it. Lonely people are restless people, and nothing will isolate us from God and from others like a life of sin.

But Jesus Christ can take care of that sin problem for us. He said, "Come unto me . . . and I will give you rest."

Rest is not a goal that we achieve by our own efforts. Rest is a gift that we receive from Jesus Christ. It is not a matter of doing something religious, or remodeling certain areas of your life. It is not by giving up this or avoiding that. No, this rest that we so desperately need can be obtained in only one way: we must receive Jesus Christ into our hearts as Lord and Savior; and when we have Christ, we have His rest. Either sin and self rule our lives and we are restless, or Christ rules our lives and we have peace. There is no middle ground.

God's way of salvation is simple, but it is not easy or

38

cheap. For Christ to be able to give us rest meant that He had to go through the agony of Calvary. It meant yielding His body and being nailed to that tree. It meant taking your sins and mine on His own body and suffering our judgment. The gift of rest was purchased by the blood of Jesus Christ at the cross of Calvary.

Sin is like a fever in our system; and we toss and turn, this way and that way, trying to get relief. The hymnwriter Isaac Watts puts it this way:

> So when a raging fever burns
> We shift from side to side by turns.
> And 'tis a poor relief we gain
> To change the place, but keep the pain.

No, the solution is not to "change the place." The solution is to change the heart, to turn away from sin and receive Jesus Christ. "Come unto me and I will give you rest," is His promise. The word is *come*—not *do,* or *try,* or *hope,* or *pay,* or *work. Come!* This means turning your back on the substitutes that are killing you and turning your face toward Jesus Christ, who alone can give you life and peace. It means throwing off the blistering yoke of sin and taking by faith the easy yoke of Christ, the yoke that sets you free.

"Come unto me, all ye that labor and are heavy laden, and I will give you rest. Take my yoke upon you and learn of me, for I am meek and lowly in heart, and ye shall find rest unto your souls."

This is His loving invitation to you. Will you right now accept His invitation and receive for yourself His gift of rest?

8

Why Did Jesus Die?

The trial was illegal, the charges were false, and the witnesses were paid to lie. From every human point of view, the death of Jesus Christ was a triumph of injustice and inhumanity. Yet—He died *willingly*. He could have commanded the armies of heaven to rescue Him, but He refused. Instead, He surrendered Himself into the hands of wicked men; and He willingly died on the cross. Why did Jesus? There are at least three answers to that question.

I John 4:9 gives us the first answer: "In this was manifested the love of God toward us, because that God sent his only begotten Son into the world, that we might live through him." Jesus died that we might live through Him.

The Bible pictures the condition of the sinner in many ways. Jesus compares us to lost sheep, or to sons who have rebelled and left home. We are described as prisoners, bound by the chains of our own sins, or as blind men groping about in the darkness. But often in the Bible we are compared to dead men. "The soul that sinneth, it shall die," said the prophet. "And you hath he made alive who were dead in trespasses and sins," Paul wrote in Ephesians 2:1.

The comparison between physical death and spiritual death is not too difficult to grasp. A man who is physically dead does not respond to physical things. He has no appetite for food; he has no ability to work; he does not even respond to your voice or touch. So it is with the person who is spiritually dead: he does not respond to spiritual things. He can read the Bible and see the words, but never understand the truth. He can sing hymns in a church service, but his heart does not understand them. He has no appetite for spiritual food or fellowship. The spiritually dead man does not respond to spiritual things.

Now, what does a dead man need? He needs life! Not religion, or reformation, but resurrection! And life is exactly what Christ gives us when we turn to Him by faith. "He that heareth my word and believeth on him that sent me hath everlasting life, and shall not come into judgment, but is passed from death unto life" (John 5:24). That is resurrection.

Christ died that you might live through Him. He bore the shame and penalty of our sins that He might forgive us and give us His eternal, abundant life. "Christ died for our sins according to the Scriptures."

Christ died that we might live through Him; but He also died that we might live *for* Him. "And that he died for all, that they which live should not henceforth live unto themselves, but unto him which died for them, and rose again" (II Cor. 5:15).

Selfishness lies at the root of sin. Because our first parents selfishly wanted something for themselves, they plunged the whole of humanity into sin and death. We want things to go our way and satisfy our desires. Selfishness breaks up homes; selfishness alienates friends; selfishness causes wars.

The only real cure for selfishness is love, and the only way to get this love is through Jesus Christ. "The love of God is shed abroad in our hearts by the Holy Spirit who is given unto us" (Rom. 5:5). When a person becomes a Christian, love becomes the motivating force of his life. "We know that we have passed from death unto life because we love the

41

brethren" (I John 3:14). "By this shall all men know that ye are my disciples, if ye have love one to another" (John 13:35).

Christ died my death for me that I might live His life for Him. He died to liberate me from a selfish, narrow existence, into a full and free experience of sharing with others. In Christ there is no such thing as rich or poor, bond or free, high or low. We are all one in His love.

Years ago, the Salvation Army was holding an international convention; and their founder, Gen. William Booth, could not attend because of physical weakness. He cabled his convention message to them. It was one word: OTHERS.

Are we living for others? If not, then Jesus died in vain, because He died for us that we might not live for ourselves, but for Him and for others.

Christ died that we might live *through* Him—that's salvation; and Christ died that we might live *for* Him—that's service. But there is a third reason why Jesus died. "For God hath not appointed us to wrath, but to obtain salvation by our Lord Jesus Christ, who died for us, that whether we wake or sleep, we should live together with him" (I Thess. 5:9-10). He died that we might live *with* Him.

That is what He promised His disciples that last evening before He went to the cross. "In my Father's house are many dwelling-places. I go to prepare a place for you." Jesus prayed to His Father, "Father, I will that they also whom thou hast given me, be with me where I am; that they may behold my glory" (John 17:24).

At the beginning of human history, man and God lived together in harmony. Then sin's earthquake created a vast gulf between man and God. But Jesus the carpenter built a bridge across that chasm, and through His death on the cross brought men back to God. And now as believers, we need never fear death, because Christ has promised us a home in heaven. "Surely goodness and mercy shall follow me all the days of my life, and I shall dwell in the house of the Lord forever" (Ps. 23:6).

Christ left His home that you and I might have a home.

While here on earth, He had no place that He could call home, no place to lay His head. He became poor to make us rich. He was made lower than the lowest that one day we might be lifted higher than the heavens. He went through suffering that we might share glory. He died that we might live with Him.

There is a life after death, an eternity after time. And you will spend that eternity either at home with Christ in glory, or separated from Christ in darkness and pain. Often people say, "I can't believe in a God who would prepare a place like hell for people to suffer in forever." I usually reply, "No, neither can I; because God did not prepare hell for people— He prepared it for the devil and his angels. But Christ is preparing a glorious home for those who will yield to Him."

One of these days soon, God is going to call His family home. I have a title deed to a home in heaven, not because of anything I am or I have done, but because Christ died for me and I have trusted Him as my Savior.

Jesus died that you might live *through* Him, *for* Him, and *with* Him. Are you trusting Him?

9

The Best Is Yet to Come

Jesus was no recluse. As you read the four Gospels, you see Him enjoying the hospitality of Mary and Martha at Bethany, having dinner with one of the Pharisees, and enjoying a feast at the home of Matthew the publican. In fact, the very first miracle He performed was at a wedding feast. The wine ran out and it looked as though the feast would end in embarrassment. But Jesus had the servants fill six large containers with water, and He turned the water into wine. When the leader of the feast tasted the wine, he said to the host, "You have saved the best wine until the last" (John 2:10). Did you know, my friend, that God always saves the best for the last?

It was customary in Jesus' day to serve the best wine first. Then, after the guests had filled up on the wine and good food, the host could bring out the inferior food and drink, and nobody would know the difference. But Jesus doesn't follow the customs of the world: He starts with the good, then gives the better, and finally the best. God always saves the best for last.

Now, sin doesn't work this way. Sin always starts with what appears to be the best and ends with the worst. There is pleasure in sin, but this pleasure is for a season. And the man who is enjoying sin needs to remember that the worst is yet to come! Satan knows just how to trap people. He allures them with the pleasure of sin, but he never warns them about the pain that follows. How many people with shattered minds and bodies, with broken lives, are crying out, "If only I had known that sin saves the worst till the last!"

There are many warnings against sin in the Book of Proverbs, especially against the sin of drunkenness. In Proverbs 23, King Solomon says an interesting thing. "Who hath woe? Who hath sorrow? Who hath contentions? Who hath babbling? Who hath wounds without cause? Who hath redness of eyes? They that tarry long at the wine when it is red, when it giveth his color in the cup, when it moveth itself aright. At the last it biteth like a serpent and stingeth like an adder" (vv. 29–32). *At the last*—sin always saves the worst till the last.

Here is a man out to have what he thinks is a good time. He sits and looks at his cup of wine. He admires its sparkle and beauty; he sips it and enjoys the taste. At the beginning, sin is always a pleasant thing; otherwise nobody would sin. But afterward—that's another story! Afterward, man isn't thinking about the beauty of the cup or the excellence of the taste. No, he's a sick man—he's made a fool out of himself— he has wounds on his body from the drunken brawl he started.

Sin always starts with the best but ends with the worst. In spite of inflation and devaluation, sin still pays the same wages—death. A man still reaps just what he sows. We may not see it now, but we will see it sooner than we expect—the worst is yet to come. And the day will come when we will hate ourselves for thinking that we could sin and get away with it. With sin, the worst is yet to come; but for the Christian, the best is yet to come. God always saves the best for the last.

You can see this principle operating in nature. When God made this world, He made it on the principle of growth and change. A seed isn't a very pretty thing (nobody sits and admires seeds), but a seed has the potential of becoming a beautiful flower or a useful plant. When you bury that seed in the ground, it takes root and starts to develop. But a root isn't anything beautiful, either. If that little seed could talk, it might say something like this: "Here I am an ugly seed. And if that isn't bad enough, they've buried me underground. And do you know what's happened? I've developed some ugly growth called roots. I'm just one big mass of ugliness!"

But just give yourself a little time. The spring rains, the warm sunshine, and before long, a green shoot—then leaves—then a gorgeous flower! In nature, the best is yet to come. We don't judge the seed by its smallness and plainness, or by its ugly, dirty roots. We see in it the beautiful flower that is yet to come.

This also applies to insect life. Now, I must confess to you that I am no lover of little crawling creatures. But isn't it interesting that God can take an ugly little worm and turn it into a beautiful butterfly? My heart goes out to that little worm, but I have a word of encouragement for it: the best is yet to come!

All of nature is living on the tiptoe of expectancy. Paul tells us in Romans 8 that all of creation is in travail, just waiting for Jesus to come back to deliver nature from the bondage of sin. For nature, the best is yet to come. Even with all of the beauty we see around us, our world is not the way God wants it to be. Sin has made havoc of God's glorious creation. We sing "This is my Father's world," but we know that sin and death are reigning as kings over God's creation.

But the best is yet to come. God isn't finished with this world. When Jesus Christ returns, He will cast out all that is evil and ugly and will bring in a reign of love and righteousness. And God's people will look at the new creation and say, "Thou hast saved the best wine until now." God isn't finished with us, either. One of these days soon, Jesus will return and give us new bodies and a new home, and we will be with the Lord forever.

Now, this truth encourages me. When I look at my life and

see how far short I fall, I could easily be very discouraged. But then the Lord reminds me that He hasn't *made* me yet—He's *making* me! So, instead of giving up in despair, I step out by faith and do my work with a willing heart, because I know the best is yet to come.

For many people, especially shut-ins, the hours drag by slowly. Some have to live with pain and weakness, and I'm sure that the tempter works overtime to discourage them and convince them that God has forgotten them. If that's your situation, let me give you this wonderful word of encouragement: the best is yet to come. God isn't finished with you yet, and the master craftsman should never be judged by an unfinished product. God loves you, God has a plan for your life, and God will finish what He has started. The day will come when you will look into the face of your Savior and say, "You have saved the best wine until now."

Do you know why God saves the best till the last? Well, it's not because He wants to tease us or trick us into obeying Him—like the mother who promises a big dessert to the child who eats his spinach. No, it's not like that at all. God saves the best till the last so we can grow in our spiritual character and really enjoy the best when it comes. God doesn't want us to be spoiled children who get too much too soon. He wants us to grow in character and in spiritual appreciation. He starts with the good—then He gives the better—then He gives the best. One reason God is permitting trials and difficulties today is that we may be prepared to appreciate and enjoy the blessings of tomorrow.

Don't run ahead of God—let Him direct your steps. He has His plan and He has His time. God's clock is never one minute early or one minute late—it always strikes right on time. The heart of man cannot conceive the wonderful things that God has prepared for us. The best is yet to come. And when it comes, we will look back at the difficulties of life and say, "It's been worth it all."

10

Unfailing Faithfulness

No book in the Bible has more sorrow in it than the Book of Lamentations. Its very name means "to cry aloud in despair." Its author is the weeping prophet, Jeremiah; and its theme is the tragic destruction of Jerusalem. Yet this dark and gloomy book glitters with wonderful promises, such as this one: "His compassions fail not; they are new every morning: great is thy faithfulness" (3:22-23).

Regardless of circumstances, we can be sure of the faithfulness of God. God is not fickle; God does not change. He is the same yesterday, and today, and forever; and His faithfulness never fails. If for one second God ceased to be faithful to His Word and His divine nature, the whole universe would fall to pieces.

The prophet Jeremiah went through an experience that made it difficult for him to believe in the faithfulness of God. For one thing, the leaders of his day turned away from God. Even the religious leaders were trusting idols instead of the true God. The holy city of Jerusalem was a haven for false gods. Jeremiah watched his nation decay, and he knew that judgment was going to come.

Judgment did come. The Babylonian armies swept down to Jerusalem and began to destroy the city. First they captured the choicest citizens and sent them away to Babylon. Then they began to burn the holy city and the holy temple. Jeremiah lived to see his beloved nation and city fall into the polluted hands of the idol-worshiping Gentiles. He heard the arrogant Babylonian soldiers say, "Where is your God? If your God is so strong, why doesn't he deliver you? Our gods have given us the victory."

It would have been easy for Jeremiah to question the faithfulness of God at a time like that. But he didn't. As he watched the soldiers ravage the city—as the temple went up in smoke and the city walls fell down into rubble—Jeremiah looked up to heaven and said, "Great is thy faithfulness." Jeremiah knew, as you and I must know, that God is faithful in spite of the circumstances of life. In fact, the very destruction of the city was proof of the faithfulness of God. God had warned them in His Word that judgment was coming, and He was faithful in keeping His promise.

Many times in the Bible we are reminded of the faithfulness of God. Every time you see a rainbow after the storm, you see a reminder of God's faithfulness. God made a promise that He would never again destroy mankind with a flood, and He has kept that promise. He promised that the seasons would come and go with regularity, and He has kept that promise. King Solomon was able to look back over a thousand years of history, from Abraham to his own day, and say, "There hath not failed one word of all God's good promise" (1 Kings 8:56).

God is *faithful to save* all who call upon Him. "For whosoever shall call upon the name of the Lord shall be saved" (Rom. 10:13). No person ever has to wonder whether or not God will save him. God is not a temperamental judge who must be pampered into saving the lost. God is a loving Father who gave His own Son on the cross that we might have everlasting life. God is not willing that any should perish; and you can trust Him, because He is faithful to save.

He is *faithful to sympathize.* Jesus is called our "merciful

49

and faithful high priest" (Heb. 2:17). God is never too busy to listen to your problems or to help you carry your burdens. The eyes of the Lord are upon the righteous and His ears are open to their cries. When our children were small and used to play in the backyard, my wife and I would always keep our ears tuned to what was going on behind the house. God never slumbers or sleeps; He is faithful to hear our prayers and give us the strength and courage that we need.

God is *faithful to forgive.* "If we confess our sins, he is faithful and just to forgive us our sins and to cleanse us from all unrighteousness" (I John 1:9). As Christians, we shouldn't sin, but we do; and when we sin, we break our fellowship with God. We lose our joy, our power, our victory. But if we come as repentant children to the Father, and if we honestly confess our sins, He is faithful to forgive. No Christian ever has to live under the dark cloud of defeat. God is faithful to forgive.

God is also faithful to chasten. In Psalm 119:75, the writer says, "Thou in faithfulness hath afflicted me." A righteous father inflicts punishment for the good of the offender. God faithfully spanks His children when they get out of hand. "Whom the Lord loveth he chasteneth." Jeremiah knew that the fall of Jerusalem was God's way of chastening His people because He loved them. Yes, every page of the Bible gives us the same message: "Great is thy faithfulness."

One of the great men of missionary history is James Hudson Taylor, founder of the China Inland Mission. If you have never read his life story, I urge you to do so, because it is a thrilling testimony to the faithfulness of God. Hudson Taylor had a deep experience with God that taught him not to trust in himself. He wrote to a friend, "It is not a striving to have faith, but looking off to the Faithful One is all we need."

Too many of us trust our faith instead of trusting the Lord. Paul tells us that even if we believe not, God abides faithful; He cannot deny Himself (II Tim. 2:13). Victorious Christian living is not the result of great faith, so much as faith in a great God. If day by day we will depend on the faithfulness of God, He will see us through.

Take this matter of temptation. All of us are tempted. But God promises to give us victory. I Corinthians 10:13 promises, "God is faithful who will not permit you to be tempted above that you are able, but will with the temptation also make a way to escape that you might be able to bear it." It's not a matter of struggling in my own strength, but rather trusting the faithfulness of God.

The same principle applies to the testings and persecutions of life. Hebrews 10:23 says, "Let us hold fast the confession of our faith without wavering, for he is faithful that promised." There is no difficulty of life too great for the faithfulness of God. He took Israel through the wilderness; He took David through the battle; He took Daniel through the lions' den; and He can take us through our testings as well.

If you look within, you will probably see failure. If you look around, you will see frustration and fear. But if you look up, you will see faithfulness. "His compassions fail not, they are new every morning, great is thy faithfulness." With such a faithful God, we never have to fear. He keeps His Word, so we can claim His promises and rest upon them. He fulfills His purposes; so we can say, "And I know that all things are working together for good."

You and I may look around at the frightening circumstances of life and wonder whether God knows or cares. My friend, He knows—and He cares. In spite of circumstances, we can say, "Great is thy faithfulness." God is faithful; God has not changed; God is working out His purposes in our lives and in this world. No wonder the psalmist sang out: "I will sing of the mercies of the Lord forever: with my mouth will I make known thy faithfulness" (Ps. 89:1).

11

The Art of Interior Decorating

Whenever I have the time, I enjoy browsing in secondhand bookstores. One day I was scanning the shelves in a bookstore in Cincinnati, Ohio, when I discovered a volume out of place. It was in the "Religion" section, but the title of the book was *The Art of Interior Decorating.* I started to remove the book, but then it dawned on me that the volume was just where it belonged. For, after all, isn't that what the Christian faith is all about—interior decorating?

I can't think of a better description of the Christian life than "interior decorating." You see, the Bible emphasizes the fact that each of us has an "inner man"—the real person down inside. The body may change and decay and even die, but the "real you" down inside will live forever.

Now, the inner man of the unsaved person is dead. The unsaved man is alive physically and aware of the visible world around him, but he is dead spiritually and cut off from the invisible world of spiritual things that he so desperately needs. This is why Jesus said to that respectable religious leader, Nicodemus, "You must be born again" (John 3:7). He meant by that statement that the inner man must be made

52

alive by God's Spirit if the person ever hopes to enter God's kingdom.

This helps to explain why Jesus had to die in order to save us. He had to pay the price for sin, which is death, in order that every barrier might be removed between your inner man and God. Once our sins are forgiven, then God can move into our inner man and make us alive spiritually. By receiving Christ as Savior, you experience new life within; and you really begin to live.

But this is only the beginning. Once we have surrendered to Christ and received eternal life by faith, then we cooperate with Him in this important job of "interior decorating." Being born again isn't the end—it's the beginning. The apostle Paul puts it this way: "For the grace of God that bringeth salvation hath appeared to all men; teaching us that, denying ungodliness and worldly lusts, we should live soberly, righteously, and godly in this present world" (Titus 2:11-12). God's grace not only redeems us, but God's grace also reforms us. Our bodies are the temple of God, and certainly we want our bodies to be fit habitations for His Spirit. We need to be busy beautifying our lives to the glory of God.

Several times in the Book of Psalms we find the interesting phrase "the beauty of holiness." To many people today, there is no real beauty in holiness. They associate the word *holiness* with unhappy people who never smile, who never have any fun, and who are difficult to get along with. Many people consider a holy life as something abnormal and out of date.

When Jesus was ministering here on earth, He discovered that the common people had the wrong idea of holiness or righteousness. They looked at the Pharisees, for example, and considered them to be holy men; and yet Jesus condemned the Pharisees as play-actors and counterfeits. Their so-called righteousness was simply an outward performance to be seen of men. There is certainly nothing beautiful about hypocrisy!

In the Sermon on the Mount, Jesus makes it very clear that true righteousness comes from within, from a surrendered heart. In the Beatitudes, for example, He emphasizes inward attitudes—being poor in spirit, being sorry for sin, showing mercy, thirsting after purity—and then He explains that these inward attitudes will change our outward actions. In other words, *when the heart is beautiful toward God, the life will be beautiful toward men.* This is the "beauty of holiness"—not an artificial masquerade that we practice, but a sincere openness toward God that makes us more like Jesus Christ.

"The beauty of holiness": this is an inner beauty that comes from God . . . a beauty that grows day by day and makes us easier to live with, and that makes us more effective as witnesses for Jesus Christ. "Let your light so shine before men," said Jesus, "that they may see your good works, and glorify your Father which is in heaven" (Matt. 5:16). And the apostle Peter wrote to Christian wives that they should not go overboard on fashions and fads, but rather cultivate the adorning of a "meek and quiet spirit" (I Peter 3:1-4).

Perhaps some of us need to start thinking about our interior decorating. All of us are careful about our exterior decorating. We spend hours every week making ourselves look as presentable as possible, and this is good. But we must remember the warning of God's Word: "Man looketh on the outward appearance, but the Lord looketh on the heart" (I Sam. 16:7). As God looks on your heart, what does He see? Jealousy? Hatred? Unconfessed sin? Fear? What kind of pictures hang on the walls of your mind? If there is a need for some redecorating, let me assure you that Jesus Christ can do the job, if you will let Him.

The thing that makes a house what it is, of course, is the character of the tenants who live inside. I know a family that moved into a house that had been allowed to run down disgracefully. The house needed paint as well as general repairs, and was ready to become an eyesore in the neighborhood. But when the new tenants arrived, things began to change. The weeds were pulled out of the yard. The house was cleaned and repaired. The trim and the shutters received a badly needed paint job; and before long, the house was beautiful again.

So it is with our lives. When Jesus is permitted to move

into our hearts and take control, then everything starts to change. He puts a new heart within us so that we have a hunger for purity and not for sin. He begins to renew our minds so that we think God's thoughts after Him. He gradually overcomes old habits and replaces them with new habits of kindness and love. In short, He becomes the "spiritual interior decorator" of our lives.

Like any workman, Christ uses tools to accomplish the job. His tools are the Bible, prayer, worship, Christian fellowship, and suffering. As you read the Bible, its truths go to work in your heart and mind and, in a wonderful way, they change you. As you pray, the Holy Spirit works within and strengthens you. As you worship God, His glory grows within. Christian fellowship, too, helps to remove old ugliness and apply new beauty. And even in suffering, God polishes our lives and makes them more attractive. Some of the most beautiful people I have ever known have gone through suffering and trial, and this is what has made them what they are.

Let's not be satisfied simply with being saved, as wonderful as that is. Let's concentrate on the "interior decorating" and ask the Lord to make our lives beautiful for His glory. The pollution picture in our world today is an ugly one; but I fear that polluted air, land, and water are but the results of polluted lives. Only Jesus Christ can make lives beautiful, and then, through them, help to make a more beautiful world. And, one of these days soon, when Jesus comes back, He will finish the decorating job—and "we shall be like him, for we shall see him as he is" (I John 3:2).

12

The Medicine of a Merry Heart

A doctor friend of mine used to cry on my shoulder occasionally. One day he said to me, "You know what's wrong with this world? I'll tell you what's wrong—people expect me to solve their problems with pills. All you can do is relieve the symptoms, but the problems are still there." Then he added, "If people would just live right, they'd feel better." His statement reminded me of something Solomon wrote in the Book of Proverbs: "A merry heart doeth good like a medicine" (17:22). Have you ever thought about the healing power of happiness?

There is a joy from God that heals. All of us know from experience that bad news makes us feel sick, but good news makes us feel pleasant all over. All of us have friends who refresh us and make us feel better for having been with them. And, sad to say, all of us know people who seem to live in the shadows, who always bring a minor note of gloom into the symphony of life.

To be sure, there is a note of sadness in the world because sin is in the world. But there is also a note of gladness. The bird sings the loudest in the storm. There is beauty and peace

56

even in a winter landscape. No matter how dark the day, God gives us joy; and no matter how lonely the night, God gives us a song. Christians have every reason to cultivate a merry heart. Our sins have been forgiven. Christ has written our names down in heaven. He is preparing us a home in heaven. He has promised to come to receive us and take us to glory. Of all people, we Christians ought to have a merry heart.

I suppose that temperament does have something to do with a person's outlook on life, and perhaps there are physical causes as well. But I sincerely believe that God wants us to have a merry heart, an optimistic outlook on life. Now, I'm not talking about foolish jesting or worldly humor; I'm talking about that overflowing joy within that is the birthright of every Christian.

Some Christians may not know the difference between being sober and being somber. All Christians should be sober and take life seriously; but I don't believe God wants us to be somber—to have a gloomy, dismal attitude. In fact, Jesus condemned this kind of attitude when He saw it in the lives of the Pharisees. He warned us in the Sermon on the Mount not to have a long face, a sad countenance, just so people will think we are spiritual. Nothing will drive people away from Christ faster than a church full of sad looking people.

No, the Lord wants us to have joy. Paul reminded Timothy that God gives us "richly all things to enjoy" (I Tim. 6:17). When the prodigal son came home and was forgiven, the father gave him a feast. The Bible says, "They began to be merry." There is joy in heaven when even one sinner repents, and certainly God's will should be done on earth as it is in heaven. Solomon was right—"A merry heart doeth good like a medicine." Not the artificial, worked-up, foolish laughter of this world, but the sincere, spiritual joy that we have in Christ because our sins have been forgiven. The best way to stay spiritually healthy is to take the right medicine, "A merry heart doeth good like a medicine."

Jesus is known as "The Man of Sorrows"; yet I submit to you that nobody ever experienced deeper joy than He did. We have in the New Testament records of at least three instances when Jesus wept; we have no record that He laughed, but I am sure He did. Jesus went through all the normal experiences of life so that He could be my sympathetic and understanding high priest; and I simply cannot conceive of Jesus never laughing.

In fact, as you read His sermons and parables in the Gospels, you detect a keen sense of humor. A father was conducting family devotions one day and was reading from Matthew 23, Jesus' denunciation of the Pharisees. At one point his son laughed out loud. The father was upset. "There's nothing funny about this," he said to his son. "But there is, daddy," said the boy. "Just think of how funny it is to strain out gnats and swallow camels!" and at that the whole family broke out laughing.

Of course, the humor in the Bible is not like our Western humor. Oriental people laugh at the ridiculous, at contrasts that are so obvious they are simply funny. I'm sure the crowd that listened to the Sermon on the Mount must have chuckled when Jesus described the man with a log in his eye who was trying to get a speck out of his brother's eye. And when Jesus compared the stern, religious Pharisees to whitewashed tombs, the crowd must have laughed out loud. Certainly the Bible is not a joke book, but it does use humor to get its message across. And the Bible recommends a merry heart as the medicine to heal the spiritual illnesses of life.

To begin with, we must learn to laugh at ourselves. It's possible to take ourselves too seriously. More than once I have seen innocent laughter relieve tension and open the way toward solving problems. As a pastor, I have sometimes made suggestions in committee meetings and discovered that the suggestions were ill-timed. The temperature began to go down and the atmosphere became tense. At those times I have had sense enough to laugh at myself and admit my mistake; and the laughter has always come like medicine to heal whatever wounds were caused.

A missionary executive once told me that he would never appoint a missionary who didn't have a sense of humor. "It's just too hard out there on the field," he told me. "The workers who can laugh at themselves are the ones who last."

"A merry heart doeth good like a medicine." But what is the secret of a merry heart?

Aren't some people born with a pessimistic outlook on life? Possibly so, but when a person is born again, a new nature comes in and with it comes a new outlook on life. I think the reason many people do not have a merry heart is because they have never been born again—they don't look at life through the eyes of faith.

Wherever Jesus looked, He saw the hand of God. The lilies reminded Him that God clothes us; so we don't have to worry about that. When He saw the sparrows, He remembered that God feeds us, too. Jesus lived each day in the realization that His heavenly Father was taking care of Him. This is one of the secrets of a merry heart—the wonderful truth that God is on the throne watching over His children. As long as we are doing His will, everything in the universe is working for us. When you know this, you can face each new day and say to your heart, "This is the day which the Lord hath made, we will rejoice and be glad in it" (Ps. 118:24).

The second truth that makes for a merry heart is this: joy comes from serving others. You don't get a merry heart by going out looking for it, because happiness is a by-product of service. The most miserable people I know are those who think only of themselves. The happiest people I know are those who think of others. Selfishness always smothers happiness. It's one of the killjoys of life. But sacrifice and service open the springs of God's happiness and flood our hearts with joy.

When I find that my own supply of joy is rather low, I take time to read the Bible and pray. Fellowship with God is sure to give me a merry heart. Jesus said, "Abide in me . . . that your joy may be full" (John 15:10-11).

Of course, a merry heart is not something we keep to ourselves. Like any medicine, it must be applied. We must share our joy with others. Some people are like poison and some are like medicine. Some bring you a feeling of death and others bring the excitement of life. When a Christian is filled with God's Spirit, he radiates love and joy and peace. His heart is joyful in the Lord, and that joy is medicine to your heart. No matter what kind of disposition we were born with, the Holy Spirit can create within us a new heart and a joyful spirit.

I don't know about you, but I would rather go through life with a merry heart, sharing with others the joy of the Lord, than anything else I can think of. Our world is filled with so much sorrow and pain. Why not ask God to give you a merry heart so that you, too, can make life easier and happier for others?

13

The Blessing of Not Knowing It All

The wiser a man becomes, the more ignorant he knows himself to be. All of us come to a certain point in life—usually when we are younger—when we feel that all wisdom is ours and there is just nothing more to learn. Then we turn a corner and discover that our store of knowledge is just a little puddle on the shore, and that a vast and deep ocean lies before us. It's good for us to remember the simple statement that the apostle Paul makes in I Corinthians 13: "For we know in part." There is a blessing in not knowing it all!

"For we know in part." Paul makes that statement in his famous poem on love. He wrote to a group of people who boasted in their knowledge. Unfortunately, they didn't have love; and so they used their knowledge to tear down and not to build up. "Knowledge puffs up," Paul warned them, "but love builds up." Then he reminded them that they really didn't know as much as they thought they knew: "For we know in part."

When you and I realize the truth of this statement, it will bring some very practical benefits to our lives.

For one thing, it will keep us humble; and humility is an

important factor in a happy, holy life. All of us know people who never admit their ignorance. For some reason, they think they have to know everything and be able to explain every puzzle of life or solve every problem. Well, I feel sorry for them; because the Bible says "We know in part." I don't have to act like God. I don't have to explain the mysteries of the universe or untangle the troubles of the world. There are questions I can't answer and there are mysteries I can't explain, because I know in part.

Now, this doesn't mean that we should close our minds and stop learning. Quite the opposite is true. There are many things God hasn't revealed to us, but there are many more things that He has revealed, and we should delve into these things and learn all we can. But it does us good while we study to pause and remind ourselves that we know in part.

Knowledge mixed with pride leads to tyranny and persecution, but knowledge mixed with humility generates a wonderful power for good. The fact that we know in part ought to make us easier to live with. It ought to deliver us from useless arguments about minor matters. It ought to mellow our convictions so that we can disagree without being disagreeable.

You see, the person who admits his ignorance is the one who ends up learning the most. It was Paul's pride of learning that kept him ignorant of God's simple plan of salvation. God literally had to knock Paul down—He had to humble him—before He could teach Paul the truth. And then, after Paul had experienced so many wonderful blessings, including being taken to the third heaven, God had to give Paul a thorn in the flesh to keep him humble. Humility is the secret of wisdom, and humility comes when you and I realize that we know in part.

There is a second result: the blessing of kindness toward others. The next time you are tempted to judge someone severely, remember what Paul wrote: "For we know in part."

As a pastor, I have had to be reminded of this often. More than once I have wrongfully passed judgment on another Christian without really knowing all the facts; and, I must confess, more than once I have had to confess it to God and to those involved. How quick we are to judge! We know perfectly well that "man looks on the outward appearance, but God looks on the heart"; yet we jump to conclusions and pass judgment anyway. We know that Jesus warned us, "Judge not that ye be not judged," but we go ahead and announce the verdict.

You and I don't really know what goes on in the heart of the other person. Perhaps if we knew his burdens at home—or his problems at work—or the physical pain he has to bear—I'm sure we would be more charitable and less critical. I recall with shame an experience I had in one of the churches I pastored. One of our Sunday school teachers was not at all faithful to the services of the church, although he was always present to teach his class. I said something severe about him to our superintendent, and he wisely replied: "Pastor, you've been here only a short time. You haven't had opportunity to visit in his home. Make a visit, then pass judgment."

Well, I made the visit, and my heart was broken. That man had an invalid child at home—a case so pitiful it would break your heart. Now, instead of criticizing that man, I admire him as one of the best Christians I know. I was able to love him and accept him and work with him because I better understood the burdens that he bore. The French have a proverb, "If we knew all, we would forgive all." That may not be totally true; but it does remind us to be slow to judge, because we know in part.

The blessing of humility—the blessing of kindness toward others: here are two practical benefits from admitting that we don't know it all. But there is a third benefit, one that has helped me over many a rugged road in life, and it's this: when you realize that you know in part, you are better able to accept the burdens and disappointments of life.

Romans 8:28 doesn't say, "And we *see* all things working together for good." No, it says, "And we *know* that all things are working together for good"—we know it whether we see it or not!

Many a person has wrecked his life on the rocks of disappointment, only to discover later that those same rocks could have been used as stepping-stones to greater things. Perhaps life has taken a turn for the worse for you, and you're wondering if God really cares. As you look the situation over, it seems pretty impossible, and maybe you're ready to call it quits. My friend, listen to me: we know in part. You don't see the whole picture now, and you may not see it a week from now or a year from now. But God sees it. And if you could only see the total picture as He sees it, you would shout for joy instead of weeping in sorrow.

"We know in part;" and because we do, we're not going to give up when life becomes difficult. Like Job, we will say, "Though he slay me, yet will I trust him." We will join with Paul and shout, "All things are working together for good!" With the choirs of heaven, we will sing: "Hallelujah—for the Lord God Omnipotent reigneth!"

Someone has compared life to a medical prescription. The pharmacist mixes the ingredients and produces medicine that will help you get well. If you took those ingredients separately, or if you changed the proportions, you might do irreparable damage, or even cause death. God knows how to mix the ingredients of life. We know in part, but God knows fully and completely. And one day, when we see Jesus Christ, God will show us the whole picture. Then we'll understand the meaning of the so-called tragedies of life.

Quite frankly, I'm glad that we know in part. I'm not so sure I want to know what lies at the next bend in the road. God knows the future, and that is security enough for me. God does not have to give me reasons or explanations or previews, because He has already given me promises; and His promises cover every problem of life. Jesus said to Peter, "What I do, thou knowest not now; but thou shalt know hereafter." Today, we know in part; but the day will come when we will know even as we are known—and I'm willing to wait. Never doubt in the darkness what God has told you in the light. Rest on His promises, and all will be well.

14

You Can Have a Happy Home

A cute little girl was sitting on top of a pile of luggage in a hotel lobby. Her parents were at the desk registering for their room. A sympathetic lady asked the little girl if they were visiting relatives in the city. "Oh, no," the girl replied. "We're going to live at this hotel until we find a house. My Daddy has a new job and we had to sell our house and move." The lady said, "Oh, it's too bad you don't have a home." To which the girl replied, "Oh, we have a *home*—it's just that we don't have a house to put in it."

A contractor can build you a house, a realtor can sell you a house, but only you can make a home.

Someone has said that home is the place where we're treated the best and complain the most! In his poem "The Death of the Hired Man," Robert Frost says: "Home is the place where, when you have to go there, they have to take you in." And all of us remember Edgar Guest's poem that says, "It takes a heap o' livin' to make a house a home." You can build a house out of bricks and wood and plaster; but it takes love, patience, forgiveness, and faith in Christ to make that house a home.

On the banks of the James River in Virginia, one of the early settlers erected a tombstone in memory of his wife. On it he wrote: "She touched the soil of Virginia with her little foot and the wilderness became a home." Houses are made of planks and plaster, but homes are made of people—people who love each other and who live to serve each other. Houses have a tendency to *fall apart*—they always need paint and repairs. But homes have a tendency to *grow together,* to become stronger and more beautiful.

One of the tragedies of life today is the decay of the home. Homes have turned into hotels, where people with the same name sleep and eat when they don't have something else to do. Home is a place to grab a bite to eat, change clothes, and take off for something more exciting. Someone has suggested that the ideal entrance to the modern house would be a revolving door!

Sad to say, some homes are battlegrounds. It doesn't surprise me that young people prefer staying away from home when all parents do is argue and fight. God never meant it to be that way. Home is not a place to hang your hat: it's a place to satisfy your heart. It's the place where we don't have to wear masks and pretend, but where we can be ourselves among people who accept us for what we are—and who love us just the same. Jesus compared heaven to a home (John 14:2). Home is to be a heaven on earth, but sometimes just the opposite is true.

I suppose I could check back and count up all the weddings I have officiated at in my years of ministry; I'm sure there are hundreds. And I wish I could visit all of the homes that have grown out of those marriages. If I could, I would leave at each of them one verse from the Bible. It is the verse that, to me, above all others, tells us how to have a happy home. "And be ye kind one to another, tenderhearted, forgiving one another, even as God for Christ's sake hath forgiven you" (Eph. 4:32). This is the very heart of happiness in our homes.

A happy home does not depend on externals—furniture,

clothes, swimming pools, and things like that. A happy home depends on the hearts of the people who live there. No amount of furniture or luxuries can make up for a selfish heart or a mean disposition. We parents are sadly mistaken if we think we can build good homes out of bad hearts. We must begin with our own hearts and make sure that they are right with God. Then we can lead our children to be what God wants them to be.

"Be ye kind one to another." Kindness in the home is so important. How easy it is for us to think only of ourselves and what we want, and not to think of others. The kind word, the kind deed—these weave into the fabric of the home a beautiful picture of love. The kind person is gentle and considerate. A few years ago, my children complained about their dentist. I had gone to him myself, so I knew he was a capable man; but they were unhappy. Then the truth came out: he was a good dentist, but he wasn't kind. Well, we changed to a different dentist; and the family was very happy, because the new man had a kind, delicate touch.

"Be ye kind one to another, tenderhearted." A tender heart always means a kind touch. The opposite of tender-hearted is hardhearted, and a person with a hard heart is always hard to live with. To be tenderhearted means to exercise love and patience when dealing with others. Love is the oil that lubricates the machinery of the home. A tender heart means a loving word, patience, and encouragement. How easy it is for our children to get discouraged; and when they come home, they need some love and encouragement. Tenderhearted . . . it isn't difficult to be kind when you have a tender heart.

"And be ye kind one to another, tenderhearted, forgiving one another." There never was a happy home without for-giveness. At almost every wedding I perform, I ask in my prayer that God will give to the couple the grace of forgive-ness. It's amazing how the clouds are lifted and the barriers removed when somebody says, "I'm sorry," and somebody answers, "I forgive you." And yet I meet many people whose minds are like computers: they remember every mistake, every unkind thing; and they hold these things over other members of the family like clubs. It's next to impossible to live with somebody who doesn't know how to forgive and forget.

A kind heart, a tender heart, a forgiving heart: this is the heart of the home. But this kind of a heart is not natural to man. Our hearts are selfish and hard and often mean. It is only through Jesus Christ that we can have the kind of heart that makes for happiness in the home. And this is the kind of heart God gives you when you turn from sin and trust Jesus Christ.

Why should we be kind to one another? Because God has been kind to us. Christian love is simply treating others the way God has treated us. As we live together, we learn more about the kindness of God. Children who grow up in an atmosphere of love and kindness will soon learn to appreciate the love of God. A college student said to me, "I have a hard time thinking of God as a heavenly Father. You see, my own father was such a tyrant that the word *father* almost makes me cringe." We exercise kindness, tenderness, and forgiveness because this is the way God deals with us. Because God has been so kind and forgiving toward me, I cannot help but be kind and forgiving toward others. And the place to start is at home.

Suppose God started treating you and me the way we treat others? Suppose He acted toward His children the way we act toward our children? Would we enjoy life? I think not. God is tender toward us—patient—loving—forgiving—kind. And because He is, He expects us to act the same way toward those we live with and work with each day. If you have experienced the love and grace of God in your own heart, then you should have no trouble sharing that love with others.

"And be ye kind one to another, tenderhearted, forgiving one another even as God for Christ's sake hath forgiven you." Here we have the secret of a happy home. If Christ is in our hearts and in our homes, then He will make our homes a heaven on earth. Yes, it takes "a heap o' livin' to make a house a home"—but it also takes a heap of loving: love that is kind, tender, forgiving. Let's ask God to put that kind of love in our hearts and in our homes.

15

What Is God Like?

A happy couple arrived home from the hospital and put their new little baby into its crib. The baby's older brother tiptoed up to the crib and whispered excitedly: "Quick, little brother, before you forget—what does God look like?"

I doubt that he received any reply; but years ago, a perplexed man asked the same question of Jesus Christ. "Show us the Father," he said, "and it will satisfy us" (John 14:8). Jesus replied, "Have I been so long time with you and you don't know me? He that has seen me has seen the Father." What does God look like? He looks like Jesus Christ!

"He that has seen me has seen the Father." Jesus made that statement, and no other person would ever dare to make it. But what a revelation it gives to us of the God that we worship. When you look at Jesus Christ, you see God. The apostle John wrote, "No man hath seen God at any time; the only-begotten Son who is in the bosom of the Father, he hath declared him" (John 1:18).

You can look at the world around you and the galaxies

above you and know that there is a God. "The heavens declare the glory of God and the firmament showeth his handiwork." Creation shouts at us that there is a God, a God wise enough to plan this amazing world and powerful enough to create it and keep it going. Certainly God reveals Himself in nature whether you use the microscope or the telescope. His footprints are seen on the mountains and His fingerprints on the atoms.

But nature gives an incomplete revelation of God. For one thing, nature itself is in the bondage of sin. Paul writes that all of creation is groaning and travailing in pain, waiting to be delivered from bondage (Rom. 8:22). I saw a book in a library one day called *The Backyard Jungle.* In it the author shows that everyone of us has a jungle in his own backyard. If you could get close enough to nature, you would see fang and claw—the struggle for survival—hidden behind all the beauties we admire. Nature tells me that God exists, and that He is a God of wisdom and power. But nature tells me very little about the love of God or the grace of God.

This is where Jesus Christ comes in. Jesus is the final and supreme revelation of God, because Jesus Christ is God in human flesh. "He that hath seen me hath seen the Father." When you read the four Gospels and watch Jesus Christ in His life on earth, you are seeing a revelation of what God is like. He takes up a little child in His arms. He stops to listen to the needs of a beggar. He heals the sick. He forgives the sinful. He attends a wedding feast. He goes to a house where death has come and brings comfort. This is God: helping people like us to carry the burdens of life.

It's rather interesting that Jesus Christ attracted different kinds of people. The sinners flocked to hear Him because they knew He loved them, understood their needs, and could help them find peace. Many people today have the idea that God is interested only in religious people and has no time for sinners. But if you look at Jesus Christ, you will see how wrong that idea is. "I came," said Jesus, "not to call the righteous, but sinners to repentance." In other words, since we cannot find our way to God because of our sins, God has come down to find us! "The Son of man is come to seek and to save that which is lost" (Luke 19:10).

When you look at Jesus Christ, you begin to realize that God is a God of love, and that He is concerned about each of us individually. He is concerned about *you*.

But there is another aspect to the character of God revealed in Jesus Christ, and it's this: God is holy. Jesus loved sinners, and He forgave them; but Jesus hated sin and did His best to destroy it. For example, Jesus went into the Jewish temple and drove out the merchants who were using it for a religious supermarket. "My house shall be called a house of prayer for all nations," said Jesus, "and you have made it a den of thieves." When you see Jesus cleansing the temple, you see God with a whip in His hand. Why? Because God hates sin. God is holy.

There is a tendency today for men to make God after their own image. I recall talking to a man about spiritual things, and he raised the question of eternal judgment. He said to me, "Now, pastor, I have three children, and they don't always obey me. I could never punish my children forever just because of the few little mistakes they make. And surely God has more love than I do." Of course, my answer was that God does not condemn His own children. "God is not willing that any should perish, but that all should come to repentance." But if men refuse His grace, they seal their own doom. Certainly God is more loving than we are—but He is also more righteous than we are. He sees sin as it really is, and He will not close His eyes to sin.

"God is love"; but the Bible also says that "God is light." God's love is a holy love, and for this reason God must punish sin. But Jesus Christ makes it clear that God loves us so much that He is willing to bear our punishment for us. Nobody can find fault with God or with His wonderful plan of salvation. When you see Jesus Christ hanging on the cross, you see a God who loves you so much that He is willing to suffer your hell in your place. The ultimate revelation of

God's great love is not that flower in the garden, or those stars in the sky, but His Son hanging on the cross.

I don't know what comes to your mind when you think about God. Perhaps you see Him as a faraway governor, ruling the universe; or as a heavenly tyrant, making men miserable. Both of these concepts are false. Look at Jesus Christ and you will see a God who loves you, a God who died for you.

The more you know about God, the better you will understand yourself and the world you live in. Too many people live in fear and bondage because they simply don't understand God. They are hiding from a God who, to them, is a policeman or a judge, when they should be running into the arms of a loving heavenly Father. When you trust Jesus Christ as your Savior, He puts his Holy Spirit in your heart; and the Spirit says, "Abba Father." That word *Abba* actually means "papa," and it shows how close the Father comes to us (Rom. 8:15-16).

Jesus saw His Father at work in the everyday affairs of life. He saw God's generosity in the beauty of the flowers. Jesus said, "If your Father does this much for weak flowers, how much more will he do for you?" He saw the Father's care in the fall of a tiny sparrow. "Are not two sparrows sold for a farthing?" He asked. "And one of them shall not fall on the ground without your Father. . . . Fear ye not therefore, ye are of more value than many sparrows" (Matt. 10:29). Of Jesus' many statements, one that is particularly meaningful to me is this: "If ye, being evil, know how to give good gifts unto your children; how much more shall your heavenly Father give good things to them that ask him?" (Luke 11:13).

Those of us who know Christ by faith can have peace in the midst of a dangerous, confused world. We have a Father in heaven who knows our needs and who is infinitely concerned for our welfare. "Don't be anxious and troubled about what you shall eat, or what you shall drink, or what clothing you will wear," said Jesus. "For your heavenly Father knows that you have need of all these things."

Now, you can't call God your Father unless you are one of His children. For some reason, my mother and father were always "ma" and "pa" to the children in our neighborhood. Our house was the neighborhood gathering place, and it wasn't unusual for a dozen or more children to be playing there. I recall one day a salesman coming to the door and being shocked when all those children started calling my mother "ma." She explained, of course, that only four of the children were hers; and that if he would wait long enough, he would hear the other mothers calling their own children home.

Well, men may call God "Father," but do they really belong to His family? I can call Him "Father" because I know I am one of His children. "But as many as received him [Jesus Christ], to them gave he the privilege to become the children of God, even to them that believe on his name" (John 1:12). Jesus Christ came to reveal God. Christ revealed God in His life, His teachings, and most of all, His death on the cross. He revealed Him as a heavenly Father who hates sin but who loves sinners and forgives them when they come in repentance and faith. Christ has revealed God to us, and in this revelation is forgiveness and life.

16

Turning Mountains into Molehills

A friend of mine hiked to the top of Mount Whitney, and while coming down the mountain, had a startling experience. At fourteen thousand feet, he looked down the trail and thought he saw a man with a white cane. Surely a blind man would not be climbing a mountain! But there he was—a blind man with a white cane. With him was a fellow hiker who was describing to the blind man the rock formations and the dazzling scenery around them. After reading my friend's letter, I thought to myself, "That blind man certainly knew how to turn mountains into molehills!"

Of course, the man could have taken a much easier way. He could have stayed home in an easy chair and felt sorry for himself; or he could have turned on the radio and listened to a lecture on mountain climbing. But he didn't take the easy way; he decided to go climb the mountain. By overcoming his handicap, he turned his mountain into a molehill.

Now, most of us do just the opposite; we're very gifted at making mountains out of molehills. The least little thing becomes a gigantic problem for us. Nobody has the problems that we face! Nobody ever had the handicap that we have!

Our situation is positively the worst case on record! We allow our handicaps to master us, when we should be mastering our handicaps. We take what we think is the easy way, when we should be out there climbing that mountain.

All of us have one kind of handicap or another. Some have physical handicaps that everybody can see; others have hidden handicaps known only to them and God. Some carry family burdens; others have mental or emotional needs that keep them from living life at its best. Nobody is perfect and nobody is free from burdens of one kind or another. The important question is not "Do I have a handicap?" but rather "What is my handicap doing to me?"

I think, for instance, of our senior citizens—our "Senior saints"—some of whom are confined in hospitals or in a rest home. Here are dear people accustomed to an active life of going places and doing things, and now they must adjust to a whole new way of life. Or, I think of active people who have been laid aside by accident or injury, who may never return to what you would call "normal life" again. As you read this book, you may be confined to a wheelchair or a hospital bed; or perhaps surgery has forced you to change your whole way of life.

How are you and I going to deal with our handicaps? Are we going to resent them, rebel against them, and become angry with God? Are we going to spend the rest of our days huddled in a corner, making ourselves and everybody around us miserable? We can do this if we wish, but it certainly won't solve the problem. It will only make it worse. No, the thing for us to do is what that blind man did out in California: we need to get up, lay aside our self-pity, and go out and climb that mountain! The happiest people I know are not those who seem to have no problems in life. The happiest people I know are those who have used their handicaps to climb higher, who by faith in the Lord have turned their mountains into molehills.

Somehow we have the idea that the people in the Bible were special people, different from us today; but such is not the case. Just about everyone you meet on the pages of the

Bible had to overcome a handicap before God could use him. In more than one case, God deliberately gave believers handicaps, and this became the making of them.

I think, for example, of Jacob, the schemer, the man who always had a neat trick up his sleeve and never let anybody get the best of him. Had Jacob continued in his self-sufficient way, he would have been a failure. But one night God came down and wrestled with Jacob, and God gave Jacob a handicap: a limp. That wrestling match was the turning point of his life, and that limp was a constant reminder to Jacob that God was in control of his life.

When God called Moses, Moses argued and did his best to change God's mind. "I'm slow of speech," said Moses. "I'm not able to challenge Pharaoh or preach to Israel." But God gave him strength and grace, and Moses turned his mountain into a molehill.

And what about the apostle Paul? "And lest I should be exalted above measure through the abundance of the revelations, there was given to me a thorn in the flesh, the messenger of Satan, lest I should be exalted above measure" (II Cor. 12:7). Many Bible students believe that Paul's thorn in the flesh was eye trouble; and what a handicap that would be for a student, a writer, a preacher, a traveler! But Paul faced his mountain with faith, and God helped him climb that mountain and make it into a molehill.

I enjoy reading biographies, and it's quite revealing to discover the weaknesses of great men. Each man that God has used in a special way has carried his own particular burdens, has known his own personal handicaps. Each one faced a mountain, and with God's help, climbed that mountain to new heights of victory and ministry.

There's an interesting promise from God in Isaiah 41:14-15: "Fear not, thou worm Jacob. . . . I will help thee, saith the Lord. . . . Behold, I will make thee a new sharp threshing instrument having teeth: thou shalt thresh the mountains, and beat them small, and shalt make the hills as chaff." Imagine a little worm disposing of a great mountain! Well, you and I are like worms—weak, helpless, small; but

77

God can give us the power and courage that it takes to face those mountains and turn them into dust.

Don't permit that handicap in your life to hold you down, to make a victim out of you. You and I can turn mountains into molehills if we will but follow the directions that God gives us in His Word. What is the secret of turning mountains into molehills? Well, victory begins in your heart. If our hearts are filled with rebellion and self-pity and bitterness, then we are defeated from the start. The first step in turning mountains into molehills is to accept your handicap from the hand of God and thank Him for it. That's right—thank Him for it. After all, if you know Christ as your Savior and God as your loving Heavenly Father, you need not fear the problems He permits to come to your life. God loves us too much to harm us, and He is too wise to make a mistake. So, take the first step: by faith, accept your handicap; and from your heart give thanks to God.

Of course, this doesn't mean we do nothing about changing our situation. We ought to get the best medical help if we have a physical need; but if God sees fit not to remove our handicap, then we must accept it and give Him thanks.

The second step is to dedicate our lives and our handicap to God, for Him to use as He sees fit. God can use a broken vessel, just so long as it is clean and surrendered. Paul wrote, "When I am weak, then am I strong." You and I don't have to have perfect bodies in order to be useful to God. To be sure, our bodies are God's temple and we must take good care of them; but God will never disqualify a man because of a handicap.

The third step is this: spend your life thinking of others. It is so easy for handicapped people to become self-centered and filled with self-pity. The best way I know to overcome self-pity is in service for others. When in my own ministry I feel discouraged and my studying just won't move along, I close my books and go out to minister to people personally. As I listen to others, share their burdens, and pray with them, my own needs are met.

One of the greatest ministries in the church is that of

prayer. Wouldn't it be wonderful if all the shut-in people were joined together as a great prayer band, asking God for revival and the salvation of the lost? I have a blind friend who learned to type so he could send letters to people who need encouragement. Other shut-in folks use their telephone as a means of helping others.

I don't know what God is going to do with your particular problem or handicap, but I do know that He will do something wonderful. Yield yourself to God, give Him your handicap, and He will give you His best.

17

The God Who Makes Us Again

While driving through the Appalachian region, my wife and I stopped at a pottery shop. I had never seen a mountain craftsman make pottery on the old-fashioned potter's wheel. But there he was, sitting at his wheel, forming the clay vessel between his skilled hands. As I watched, I thought of the prophet Jeremiah who went down to the potter's house. Remember what he wrote? "And the vessel that he made of clay was marred in the hand of the potter; so he made it again, another vessel, as seemed good to the potter to make it" (Jer. 18:4).

God is revealed to us in the Bible in many different figures. Supremely, of course, God is the loving heavenly Father. But He is also creator of the worlds, the Lord of Hosts who leads the armies of heaven, and the King of kings and Lord of lords. It has always been an encouragement to me to remember that God is also pictured as the potter. Jeremiah went down to the potter's house, and there he saw the way God deals with His own children. "And the vessel that he made of clay was marred in the hands of the potter; so he made it again, another vessel, as seemed good to the potter to make it."

You and I are the clay, and God is the potter. As we yield

to His skillful hands, He molds us just the way He wants us to be. It isn't the task of the clay to think up the pattern; that's the task of the potter. God has a perfect plan for each life. All that the clay has to do is simply yield by faith into the hands of the potter, and the potter will do the rest.

As Jeremiah watched the potter, he noticed that the vessel was marred. This wasn't the fault of the potter, it was the fault of the clay. The clay would not yield. Now, if you were the potter, and the clay refused to yield to your will, what would you do? I suppose most of us would throw the half-completed vessel on the trash heap and start with a whole new lump of clay. But that's not what the potter did. He kept the wheel turning, and he patiently worked with the clay. "He made it again, another vessel, as seemed good to the potter to make it." I like those four words: *He made it again.*

I think of Abraham, that great man of faith, who one day disobeyed God and left the promised land for Egypt. While in Egypt he fell into sin and lied about his wife. In fact, because of his disobedience, he almost lost his wife. What did God do to Abraham? Did God reject him and throw him on the trash heap? No, He didn't. He made him again. He gave Abraham another chance. And as a result, Abraham became a great servant of God and was known as the friend of God.

I think of Peter, that great man of courage. "Though all others forsake you," Peter said to Jesus, "I will never forsake you." Yet Peter denied the Lord three times. What did God do with Peter? He made him again. Jesus forgave Peter and restored him to his discipleship, and Peter became a great soul-winner to the glory of God.

Perhaps today you are living under a cloud of defeat and despair. Perhaps you have disobeyed the Lord and have sinned against Him. Satan is accusing you and saying, "God is finished with you!" Listen, my friend: God will forgive your sins and make you again. God isn't through with you—no need to despair. He will make you again if you will surrender to His will.

There are many people who live under the shadow of despair because they think God is through with them. Somewhere along the line they have sinned—they have failed to yield to the Lord—and now they're convinced that this is the end. They would like to get back to church, or go back to serving the Lord again; but they feel it's impossible. It's all over—they are sure that God is through with them.

A lady phoned me to share a problem one day following a radio broadcast. It seems that when she was a teen-ager, she disobeyed the Lord and did something she wasn't supposed to do. Now she was a member of a fine church, and the church had asked her to serve as a Sunday school teacher. She said, "I don't feel qualified to serve the Lord. I just can't forget what I did."

I chatted with her and said, "My friend, I don't know your name or what you did; and I don't have to know. But God knows all about it. If you have confessed your sin to the Lord, then He has promised to forgive you. In fact, Hebrews 10:17 tells us that God remembers our sins no more. He can make you again, if you will but surrender to Him." Well, when the conversation ended, she was relieved and happy again. But as I hung up the phone, I said to myself: "Think of the years of happiness and service that dear woman missed simply because she thought God was through with her. If only she had yielded to Him sooner!"

Now, please don't get the idea that God minimizes sin. You know and I know that God does chasten His children if they continue to disobey Him. There is no place for rebels in God's family. If one of His children refuses to obey and persists in deliberate sin, God does chasten and use the rod.

But the potter is patient with the clay. "He knoweth our frame; he remembereth that we are dust." If the clay refuses to yield, or if it becomes so hard the potter cannot shape it, then there is nothing to do but to put the clay on the shelf and forget it. But before that happens, the potter lovingly and patiently deals with us to bring us to the place of surrender. After all, God has quite an investment in our lives, because Jesus shed His blood to save us from our sins. This clay He is fashioning is not cheap clay. It's the most expensive material in the universe!

"So he made it again, another vessel, as seemed good to the potter to make it." This is Jeremiah's way of saying what the apostle John wrote in I John 1:9: "If we confess our sins, he is faithful and just to forgive us our sins, and to cleanse us from all unrighteousness." Now, that word *confess* does not simply mean "admit." It means more than that. The word *confess* literally means "to say the same thing." In other words, "If we say the same things about our sins that God says about them, God is faithful to His promise, and just, and will forgive our sins and cleanse us from all unrighteousness." Trying to explain our sins, or excuse our sins, will never open the door to forgiveness. We must admit them, name them as sin, turn from them, and ask God to forgive us.

Forgiveness—being made again—is not a matter of God's love or even God's grace. In I John 1:9 it says that God is "faithful and just to forgive us." What does that mean? Well, Jesus Christ paid for all our sins on the cross. We have accepted Him as our Savior. God will not hold against us the sins that Christ has died for! He is a just God, faithful to His Word. Of course, knowing that Christ died for all my sins, and that God will forgive me, is no excuse for sin. Quite the contrary. Knowing that sin nailed Jesus to the cross should make us hate sin and want to flee from it. But let's not make forgiveness such a difficult thing that we rob ourselves of this blessing. The death of Christ on the cross, and the intercession of Christ right now up in heaven, are full provision for our cleansing.

If you are defeated and discouraged because of some disobedience, please pay attention to God's Word. "So he made it again, another vessel, as seemed good to the potter to make it." "If we confess our sins, he is faithful and just to forgive us our sins and to cleanse us from all unrighteousness." Please don't punish yourself and live under a dark cloud. God will forgive—God will forget—God will bring you out into the sunlight of His blessing. He will make you again. All that He asks is that you surrender. He is the potter, you are the clay. The potter has the plan; all the clay must do is yield. Surrender to Him. Let Him make you again.

18

Getting Accustomed to It All

When you were a child, did you ever sit down at the dinner table and say, "Are we having *that* again?" Human nature hasn't changed. Centuries ago, the Jewish nation was being fed by God from heaven. Every morning for nearly forty years, God sent the little wafers of manna down to the camp of Israel. The Bible calls it "angels' food." But there came a day when the people complained, "We're tired of this manna. The same old thing every day!" Their experience points up an important truth: the danger of getting accustomed to our blessings.

God was taking care of the people of Israel. He had delivered them from the bondage of Egypt. He had taken them through the Red Sea and had defeated their enemies. They never had to worry about where to travel, because God's presence went before them to lead the way. God protected them from danger, and God provided the food and water they needed day by day.

Now, you would think that the people would be thrilled with what God was doing for them; but they weren't. They spent much of their time complaining. They complained about their godly leader, Moses. They complained about the way God led them. They complained about the way God fed them. There was a time when Moses was a great man in their eyes, but not any more. There was a time when the pillar of fire that led them was an awesome sight, but not any more. There was a time when they could hardly wait for morning to come so they could go out to gather the heavenly manna, but not any more.

Do you know what had happened to these people? The same thing that can easily happen to you and me: *they had gotten accustomed to their blessings.* The wonder was gone. What was once a daily miracle of God's love became a routine occurrence. "We're tired of this manna!" Can you imagine being tired of food that came directly from heaven? Can you imagine getting accustomed to sharing in a daily miracle? Well, it happened to them; and it is happening to people today. We have gotten used to God's blessings.

I think of our blessings as a nation. To be sure, not everything is good about our beloved country; but not everything is bad. We enjoy freedom here; yet we've gotten accustomed to it and take it for granted. Our material wealth is the greatest of any nation on earth; yet we complain because we don't have more. While we Americans are fretting over diets and trying to lose excess weight, many people in the world are trying to find enough food to keep them alive another day.

Take this matter of government. With all of its faults, our democratic way of life is still the best way; yet how many of us really participate in the responsibilities of government? Many Christians don't even bother to register so they can vote. If God withdrew from us the national blessings that we enjoy, I'm sure everyone of us would cry out and beg Him for freedom again. It's too bad that sometimes we have to lose something to appreciate it. Don't get accustomed to the blessings we enjoy as a free nation. Cherish these God-given privileges, and use them wisely.

Whenever we start taking something or someone for granted, we start complaining. For some reason, many of us actually enjoy complaining. Yet the Bible warns us, "Do all things without murmuring and complaining" (Phil. 2:14).

I think of the complaining that can go on in a home. We take for granted the blessings of the home: clean clothes, nourishing meals, money to pay the bills, opportunity to be together and enjoy family fellowship. Then something happens and we lose some of these blessings. Perhaps mother has to go to the hospital, and we discover what's involved in keeping a home running smoothly. Or perhaps the head of the house is out of work, or has to take a cut in salary, and we find out quickly that money doesn't grow on trees. It's too bad we sometimes have to lose things to appreciate them.

Sometimes we take our spiritual blessings for granted and complain about them. Do you remember when your pastor first came to your church, how grateful you were that God sent him? You listened to his messages carefully and took them to heart. But he's been with you a few years now, and he isn't really special any more. In fact, lately you've decided that he's a bit hard to listen to—his sermons are a bit too long—and maybe he's being a bit too hard on the church. The pastors at other churches are so much easier to listen to. If that's your attitude, I want to warn you: you may be guilty of getting accustomed to your blessings.

Or, let's take the matter of our own personal Christian life. Do you remember what an exciting book the Bible used to be? When you first became a Christian, reading and studying the Bible was a delight, a joy; but today, it's more of a burden, a grind. Oh, you read your Bible—that's a habit you won't change; but it just doesn't excite you anymore. And you're glad when you've finished your reading for the day so you can watch television or read some exciting novel.

It's possible to take prayer for granted. Just think of what prayer really is: fellowshiping with the God of the universe and sharing our needs with Him! Why, this privilege ought to excite us. It ought to stir us up so much that praying would be the most enjoyable and thrilling experience of the day. But with many, prayer is just a dull routine. We've gotten accustomed to our blessings, and the results in our lives are tragic.

What happens to us when we get accustomed to our blessings? I've already mentioned one sad result: we become critical and complain. But something else happens: we lose that sense of wonder that makes life enjoyable. Life becomes very mechanical, very matter-of-fact. Instead of having a childlike spirit of humility and wonder, we become cold and hard like a machine.

When you sit down at your table to eat, do you ever feel a sense of wonder that God should take care of you? Just think of all that lies behind even a little piece of bread. Think of the thousands of gallons of rain that had to fall on that field, the thousands of hours of sunshine that God had to send. Think of the harvesting, the shipping, the milling, the baking, the distributing of the loaves—and all of this so you can have your morning toast.

A few years ago I was visiting Moody Church in Chicago when "the big snow" moved in. I will always remember those three days when our great city was almost paralyzed by nearly three feet of snow. I went down to the hotel restaurant to get some breakfast; but there was very little to eat, because the delivery trucks just couldn't get through. During that time, I'm sure many people realized that they had been taking a great deal for granted.

Please don't get accustomed to your blessings. Keep that sense of awe and wonder that God is supplying your needs day by day. Live each day as though it might be the last opportunity you will have to enjoy your family, or be with your friends, or share in a church service, or read your Bible. And when you find yourself taking things for granted, don't wait for God to deal with you. Immediately ask the Lord to give you a new appreciation for old blessings. Go a little deeper into life. Open your heart wider to the love of God. Keep that sense of wonder in your life.

Sometimes God has to deal drastically with us to teach us to appreciate necessities and stop yearning for luxuries. God had to discipline Israel when they complained, and He will surely discipline us. It doesn't take much—an illness, an automobile accident, a disappointing change in plans. Sometimes God has to use deep surgery to get rid of the spiritual cancer of complaining—the loss of a job, or even the loss of a loved one.

But these things are not needed in the life of the person who is always thankful, who appreciates God's blessings and accepts them with gratitude, who is amazed day by day that God is so good to him. Keep your heart open in gratitude to God, and life will take on a new luster of joy and wonder and peace.

19

The Truth That Loves

One of the earliest lessons we learn in childhood is to tell the truth. If we disobeyed, and then lied about it, we could look forward to being punished twice—once for the disobedience, and once for the lie. How important it is to be truthful. In several of his letters to the churches Paul emphasizes the importance of the truth. "Lie not one to another," he wrote to the Colossian Christians. And to the Ephesians he wrote, "But speaking the truth in love. . ." (4:15). I like that statement—"Speaking the truth in love"—because in it God has joined two basic ideas: honesty and love. We are to speak the truth—that's honesty. But we are to speak the truth *in love.* God wants us to practice truth in love, and He also wants us to love in truth.

There are some places where you will rarely, if ever, find truth and love joined together. Have you ever been in a court of law? Do you remember when they asked you to raise your right hand and affirm that you would tell the whole truth? Did they say anything about love? Of course not. The important thing about a witness is that he tell the truth, even if the truth hurts. In a court of law, you will rarely find love and truth joined together.

Unfortunately, in some homes you will never find love and truth joined together. Sad to say, there are husbands and wives who say they love each other, yet they are pretending and covering the truth. Or, they hate each other so much that they enjoy telling the truth! You see, love without honesty is hypocrisy. But honesty without love is brutality—and I don't want either one in my home. In our homes, all of us should speak the truth in love.

God wants us to speak the truth in love. He doesn't want us to cover the truth and pretend, or stretch the truth and lie. He wants our love to be governed by truth and the truth to be governed by love. Now, this is something that cannot be done in our own natural strength. Our human nature is such that we either go to one extreme or the other. We are either very sentimental and emphasize love, or very stern and emphasize truth. It's difficult for us to reach and maintain a proper balance here.

This is where Jesus Christ enters the scene. In Christ we have a perfect blending of truth and love. When He loved, it was always a truthful, holy love. When He spoke the truth—even when He had to be stern—it was always bathed in love. When a person yields his life to Christ, then he has within him the power to speak the truth in love. He doesn't have to be a hypocrite, a pretender. He can live openly and honestly and lovingly, with Christ in control of life. And his life will be marked by truth and love.

It's very difficult for us to maintain a proper balance between truth and love. Some Christians I know are so zealous for the truth that they show no love whatsoever. They don't care who is listening or who is hurt—they're going to tell the truth! On the other hand, there are believers who are so taken up with love that they avoid the truth and try to whitewash everything. Now, both extremes are wrong. No church or home is going to be what it ought to be if the truth is ignored. You cannot build solidly on lies. On the other hand, no church or home can be happy with cold truth alone; there must also be the warmth of love.

Often I get phone calls from young pastors who are new in

the ministry. They have problems in their churches and they want counsel, and I do the best I can to help them. One problem keeps repeating itself. The pastor will say to me, "I have a member in the church who doesn't agree with me on a certain issue. It really isn't a big thing, but he's made a big thing out of it. And he tells me that he'll leave the church if I don't agree with him."

Now, lest you get critical of our churches, let me hasten to say that I meet this same problem in some of our homes. More than one wife has told me that her home is a battlefield unless she lets her husband have his own way in everything. (I've met it the other way around, too, where the wife has to have her own way.)

My friend, if you disagree with your pastor, or with someone in your home, and you feel you have the truth, be sure to temper that truth with love. It's possible to disagree without being disagreeable. It's possible for the church leaders to discuss this matter and pray about it, in true Christian love, and to grow in grace from the experience. Sometimes truth will hurt, and that's the time to ask God for an extra supply of love.

I've always appreciated the doctor and the dentist using a pain killer when they work on me. Well, love is a great pain killer. By all means be truthful and honest, but not brutally so. Instead, speak the truth in love. The greatest example of speaking the truth in love is our Savior, Jesus Christ. The Bible tells us that "God is love"; and since Jesus Christ is God, He is love. But Jesus Himself said, "I am the truth." In Christ, we have the perfect blending of truth and love. Whenever He spoke, it was the truth spoken in love. Whenever He showed love, it was honest and sincere, not artificial. Jesus spoke—and lived—the truth in love.

The only way a person can become a Christian is through truth and love. Unless we face the truth about ourselves, we will never see the need to be saved; and were it not for God's love and grace, there would be no way to be saved.

I think, for example, of that Samaritan woman whom Jesus met at the well (John 4). Jesus talked with her about water, telling her how to satisfy the deep spiritual thirst of the heart. She became interested. "Oh, give me that water!" she said. Jesus replied, "Go call your husband." He was touching the sore spot in her life, because she had been married several times and was now living with a man who was not her husband. But see how lovingly Jesus helped her face the truth. He didn't give her a lecture about morality; He didn't dwell on the sordid aspects of her empty life. No, He spoke the truth in love. And when this woman saw herself honestly, and felt the tug of the Savior's love, she believed and was saved.

The truth condemns us, but the love of God and the grace of God provide an escape from condemnation. God doesn't save us by loving us and ignoring the truth about our sins. God has to be true to Himself, for God is a holy God. In Jesus Christ, God has caused truth and love to meet each other. When Jesus died for you on the cross, truth said: "All men are sinners." But love said, "Christ died for sinners." At the cross, God speaks the truth in love; and if you will receive God's Son into your heart, you will be forgiven and become a child of God.

The reason so many people are without forgiveness and eternal life is because they will not face the truth. Instead of openly admitting their need, they make all sorts of excuses: "I'm as good as anybody in the church"; "I pay my bills and live a clean life." Because they hide behind excuses (which are really only respectable lies), they will never face the truth and be saved.

Don't be afraid of God's truth. God speaks the truth in love. He tells the truth—not to condemn, but to save. Listen to His voice as He lovingly, patiently calls you to trust Christ as your own Savior.

20

The Tragedy of Lost Opportunity

From all outward appearances, Palm Sunday was a triumph. Christ was riding into the city like a king. The crowds were praising God and honoring Jesus. Then, at the brow of the hill, Jesus stopped. He looked down and saw spreading out before Him the city of Jerusalem. And, while the crowds were singing, Jesus was weeping. Palm Sunday was not a triumph, it was a tragedy. For Jesus was saying to the citizens of that favored city, "If you had known, at least in this your day, the things which belong to your peace! But now they are hid from your eyes" (Luke 19:42). The tragedy of lost opportunity!

Jesus does not see things the way we see them. The disciples admired the temple and pointed out its magnificent stones, but Jesus called it a den of robbers. The pious religious crowd pointed to the sinners that followed Jesus and called them ugly names; but Jesus said they were only sick people needing a physician, sheep needing a shepherd. And, on Palm Sunday, the disciples pointed to Jerusalem and proudly rejoiced in its great heritage and beauty. But Jesus looked at the same city and saw a city of dead men—a city destined to be destroyed by enemy armies. "For the days shall come upon you," said Jesus, "that your enemies shall compass you around ... and lay you even with the ground ... and they shall not leave one stone upon another."

Why did Jerusalem face this tragic judgment? Because the city was uneducated? No, within her walls were some of the most intelligent men who ever lived. Was it because the city was immoral? No, other cities in that day were just as sinful, and perhaps worse. What, then, was the reason for Jerusalem's judgment? The answer is simple: she passed up her opportunity. "You knew not the time of your visitation," said Jesus. And He wept.

No city on earth was favored as much as Jerusalem. The very Son of God walked her streets and taught in her temple courts. Before her very eyes He healed the sick; and not far from her gates, He raised the dead. The people of Jerusalem were privileged to have God visit them. And yet the record tells us, "He came unto his own, and his own received him not."

The opportunity He gave them was not just one single event; He ministered for some three years. They saw Him change men and women by the power of His grace. All the evidence was there. The door of opportunity stood wide open; yet the people refused to go in. The result was defeat and destruction. They could have enjoyed peace—peace with God and peace on earth—but instead, they suffered war.

Before we condemn them too severely, however, let's examine our own lives. Has any generation been more favored than ours when it comes to spiritual opportunities? The Word of God is as available today as the daily newspaper. You can purchase a Bible for a few cents at a newsstand. You can turn on your radio or your television and hear the gospel preached and sung. The Word of God is even beamed from a space capsule as millions of TV viewers around the world watch a trip to the moon. Our generation will never be able to say, "We didn't have an opportunity." Like Jerusalem of old, we are having our day of visitation; but what are we doing with it?

Why are many people missing their spiritual opportunities today? Some people are shackled by tradition. The Jews had their own religious system and saw no need for a change. The religious leaders in Jesus' day were shocked by His ideas. The whole purpose of the Sermon on the Mount, for example, was to expose the shallowness and falseness of the traditions of the scribes and Pharisees. "Except your righteousness shall exceed the righteousness of the scribes and Pharisees," said Jesus, "you shall in no case enter into the kingdom of heaven." Human nature hasn't changed. Most people today would rather hold onto an old tradition than face a new truth; and for this reason, they miss their God-given opportunities.

Jesus made it clear that He did not come to destroy the Jewish law, but to fulfill it. Just as the apple blossom is fulfilled in the apple, and the acorn is fulfilled in the oak, so the law was fulfilled in Christ. All the Old Testament sacrifices and ceremonies have their fulfillment in Christ. Yet the people preferred to hold to their religious system and miss the exciting fulfillment found in Jesus Christ. So often the good is the enemy of the best. The law was good—the religious system was ordained by God—but it was never meant to be God's final revelation. And the citizens of Jerusalem missed their opportunity—not because they held to something bad, but because they held to something good and turned away from the best.

I think of another reason why they missed their day of opportunity: they allowed themselves to be influenced by men who were wrong. Instead of considering the facts for themselves, they permitted the "experts" to make their decisions for them. There is an interesting scene in the seventh chapter of John's Gospel that bears this out. The religious council sent some officers to arrest Jesus, and the men came back empty-handed. "Why didn't you bring Him?" the religious rulers asked. "Never man spoke like that man!" the soldiers answered. Then the rulers replied: "Are you also deceived? Have any of the rulers or of the Pharisees believed on Him?" In other words, if the important people reject Him, that settled the question. Simply because our so-called great scientists and politicians and educators are not Christians, we should not be Christians, either!

Tradition, settling for the second best, following the wrong examples: these are some reasons why people miss their God-given opportunities. There are other reasons, of course; but I think the point is clear. If we listen to God's voice, we will know our day of opportunity and seize it. But what happens to a man who misses his day of opportunity? The ancient teachers used to say that "opportunity has hair in front of his head, but the back of his head is bald." In other words, we can seize opportunity as we meet him; but once he has passed, he is beyond our grasp.

For the people of Jerusalem, missing their opportunity meant judgment. The Roman armies finally came and destroyed their beloved city and its beautiful temple. But interestingly enough, God gave the nation several years of grace before that judgment fell. On the cross, Jesus prayed for the nation: "Father, forgive them, for they know not what they do." On the day of Pentecost, and for several years afterward, the apostles and the early believers witnessed about Jesus Christ, performed mighty miracles, and extended God's invitation to the nation. Unfortunately, the leaders did not repent and believe; but multitudes of the common people believed on Christ and were saved. Then the judgment fell.

All of which leads us to a solemn truth: no man knows when the day of opportunity will end. And because no man knows, he had better take advantage of the opportunity when it comes his way. Peter writes that God is "long-suffering toward us, not willing that any should perish, but that all should come to repentance" (II Peter 3:9). But Jesus warns us. "Yet a little while is the light with you. Walk while you have the light, lest darkness come upon you" (John 12:35).

This we know for sure: opportunity comes *today*. Not yesterday; yesterday is gone. Not tomorrow; tomorrow may not come. "Now is the accepted time," says the Bible; "now is the day of salvation" (II Cor. 6:2). "Today while you hear his voice, harden not your heart" (Heb. 3:7-8).

The message of Palm Sunday is the message of peace. Jesus said, "If only you knew those things that belong to your peace!" What an opportunity He gave them—an opportunity to enjoy peace: peace with God, peace with themselves, peace on earth, good will among men. He came as God's ambassador of peace, yet they declared war. "We will not have this man to rule over us!" He came with outspread arms of love, and they nailed them to a cross. He rode into the city as their King, and they crowned Him with thorns. And as they did these things, they were blind to the awful fact that their day of opportunity was quietly passing them by.

He comes to men today, offering His grace and love, His full forgiveness. The opportunity is here. "Today is the day of salvation!" Will you bow before Him, receive Him, trust Him? Or must He turn away and weep because another day of opportunity is gone—forever!

21

Resurrection Power

Our world today is power conscious. Young people want the most power from their stereo equipment. Drivers expect the greatest amount of power from an automobile. Travelers depend on the power of great jet engines, and scientists have penetrated outer space because of the power of the atom. But the greatest power in the universe today is not found under the hood of a car or in the engine of a rocket. It is found in the greatest miracle Jesus ever performed—His resurrection from the dead. In Philippians 3:10, Paul writes: "That I may know him, and the power of his resurrection." The power of His resurrection—the power that can change your life!

What kind of power is the power of His resurrection? To begin with, it is *saving power*. Paul writes, "That if thou shalt confess with thy mouth Jesus as Lord, and believe in thine heart that God hath raised him from the dead, thou shalt be saved" (Rom. 10:9, 10). A dead Savior is no Savior at all. But we have a living Savior! The message of the gospel makes this clear: "Christ died for our sins according to the Scriptures . . . and . . . was buried, and . . . rose again the third day" (I Cor. 15:3-4).

The world has little doubt that Jesus died, but most people are not really sure that He rose again. The first lie that was told after His resurrection was that His disciples had stolen the body, but common sense tells us that such an act would be impossible. To begin with, the tomb was guarded and sealed by the authority of Rome. Those soldiers either obeyed orders or lost their lives. In the second place, the disciples did not even believe in Christ's resurrection. When He was buried, they thought that Jesus was gone forever. In fact, even after they saw Him alive, they still doubted. Certainly men with that kind of an attitude would not steal His body and try to convince others of something they didn't believe themselves. Finally, if the disciples stole His body, they were liars and pretenders. They preached that He was alive; and more than that, they lived and died as though He was alive. They had nothing to gain by fooling themselves or other people. No, we must be honest and say that the disciples did not steal Christ's body. He rose from the dead.

Well, did His enemies take His body away? The suggestion is really unthinkable, because this is the very thing His enemies were trying to prevent. And, if they had stolen His body, why didn't they produce it and prove the disciples wrong once and for all? We are forced to the logical conclusion that Jesus rose from the dead, and that the tomb did not contain His body.

He died and rose again in order to save us from sin and death. Christ was "delivered for our offenses and raised again for our justification" (Rom. 4:25). His resurrection from the dead was proof that God had accepted Christ's sacrifice for our sins. The penalty for sin has been paid, and now men can be saved through faith in Jesus Christ.

The power of His resurrection is saving power—power to save us from sin and death and judgment. He is a living Savior, who has conquered every enemy you and I will ever face. And the first step in experiencing the power of His resurrection is trusting Him to save you.

But the power of His resurrection is not only saving power, it is also *living power*. Paul gives his own personal witness in Galatians 2:20: "I am crucified with Christ, nevertheless I live; yet not I, but Christ liveth in me: and the life which I now live in the flesh I live by the faith of the Son of God, who loved me and gave himself for me." Christ liveth in me—living power!

Many people have said, "I would like to become a Christian, but I'm afraid I just can't live the life." Of course, no one is saved by imitating Christ, but by receiving Him into the heart. When we do this, then He lives out His life through us. "Christ liveth in me"—the power of His resurrection at work in our lives every hour of every day.

One day a ticket agent looked out his window and saw a man carrying several heavy suitcases, and he was walking down the middle of the railroad track. The agent ran out and stopped him. "You can't do that," said the agent. "To begin with, you might get killed; and to make it worse, you're trespassing!" The traveler explained in broken English that he had every right to walk on the track because he had purchased a ticket miles away at the other station—and he produced the ticket from his pocket. The agent carefully explained to the man that the ticket gave him the privilege of being carried on the train, and that if he would wait a few minutes the next train would arrive.

We smile at that immigrant, but many Christians have made a similar mistake. They have trusted the power of His resurrection to save them, but they have not permitted that same power to work in their lives in a practical way day by day. Paul prayed, "Now unto him [Christ] that is able to do exceeding abundantly above all that we ask or think, according to the power that worketh in us" (Eph. 3:20). Power to control our thoughts—power to discipline our bodies—power to keep us going when things are tough—power to be kind when others are mean—power to glorify God. Resurrection power is ours for the asking!

You have noticed, I'm sure, the contrast in the disciples before and after the resurrection. Before His resurrection power went to work in their lives, they were selfish, weak, fearful, and filled with unbelief. But after Christ's resurrection power took over in their lives, they were bold, loving, and full of faith and courage. The power of His resurrection is living power—available to us today.

The power of His resurrection is not only saving power and living power, it is also *dying power*. This Christ has conquered death! The glorified Savior said to the apostle John, "Fear not; I am the first and the last: I am he that liveth and was dead, and behold, I am alive for evermore" (Rev. 1:17-18). We don't have to be afraid of life or death, time or eternity, because Christ holds the keys.

> Death could not keep her prey,
>   Jesus, my Savior;
> He tore the bars away,
>   Jesus, my Lord!

The future is full of hope for the Christian because of the power of His resurrection. Listen to Peter as he writes to Christians going through the fires of persecution: "Blessed be the God and Father of our Lord Jesus Christ, which according to his abundant mercy hath begotten us again unto a living hope by the resurrection of Jesus Christ from the dead" (I Peter 1:3). Not a dead hope, but a living hope, because we have a living Christ. And Paul wrote to the believers at Thessalonica who had lost loved ones in death: "But I would not have you to be ignorant, brethren, concerning them which are asleep, that ye sorrow not, even as others which have no hope. For if we believe that Jesus died and rose again, even so them also which sleep in Jesus will God bring with him" (I Thess. 4:13-14).

The grave is not a dead-end street for the Christian. Rather, it is a highway to heaven. "Because I live," said Jesus, "ye shall live also" (John 14:19). "I am the resurrection and the life; he that believeth in me, though he were dead, yet

101

shall he live" (John 11:25). This is the power of His resurrection: the power that conquered death, the power that makes it possible for Christians to shout: "O death, where is thy sting? O grave, where is thy victory?"

In one way or another all of us have been touched by bereavement, perhaps the loss of a loved one or a friend. We don't like to talk about it; but unless Jesus returns during our lifetime, we, too, will experience death. But the believer need not fear that experience, because Jesus Christ has gone before and taken the sting out of death. This is why the Bible calls the death of a believer "sleep." It's just like going to sleep. "Yea, though I walk through the valley of the shadow of death, I will fear no evil; for thou art with me" (Ps. 23:4).

The power of His resurrection: saving power, living power, dying power. The greatest power in the universe! And this power is yours as you put your faith in Jesus Christ. "That I may know him, and the power of his resurrection."

22

The Tyranny of Things

Are you trapped in the tyranny of things? A wealthy man was moving into a new house, and his next-door neighbor happened to be a Quaker. The Quakers, as you know, believe in simplicity and plainness of life. The Quaker neighbor watched as the movers carted in numerous pieces of furniture, a great deal of clothing, and many decorative pieces. Then he walked over to his wealthy new neighbor and said in his quaint Quaker way: "Neighbor, if thee hath need of anything, please come to see me—and I will tell thee how to get along without it." Jesus would have agreed with that advice; for He said one day, "A man's life does not consist in the abundance of things that he possesses" (Luke 12:15).

When Jesus made that statement, it dropped into the crowd like an atomic bomb. Some of the people ridiculed Him and laughed out loud. Of course a man can be measured by his wealth. Everybody knows that. How else would you determine how much a man is worth?

Well, if wealth and possessions are the measure of the man, then Jesus Christ Himself is out of the running. He was born in a stable to a humble Jewish mother who was married to a poor carpenter. He Himself said, "The foxes have dens, and the birds of the air have nests, but the Son of man has no place to lay his head." He left no full safe-deposit box when He died. If happiness and success depend on things, then Jesus was miserable and defeated. But He was not! No man experienced greater joy than He did, in spite of His sufferings. And no person ever accomplished a greater piece of work than He did on the cross. "A man's life does not consist in the abundance of the things that he possesses." Jesus preached that and practiced it, and His life proves that it is true.

Jesus knew that there are some things a man simply has to have. "Your heavenly Father knows that you have need of these things," He said in His Sermon on the Mount. Men need food, and clothing, and shelter. These are needs, and God supplies these needs. God created *things* to be used for the benefit of mankind; He did not create *things* to be worshiped as gods. And this is where the trouble lies today: too many people think that life can be built on the things that money can buy, and they forget about the things that money cannot buy. It's wonderful to have the things that money can buy, provided you haven't lost the things that money cannot buy.

I remember talking with a lovely lady whose home was about to break up. She wore expensive clothing, but underneath was a broken heart. She had a valuable diamond ring on her finger, but there was no love attached to it. She lived in a beautiful house, but for years there had been no home. Her life had been built on things that money can buy—prices, not values—and now everything was about to slip right through her fingers.

Let me make it clear: there is nothing wrong with enjoying the good things God has given us, provided they do not become substitutes for the best things of life. Henry David Thoreau was not far off when he wrote, "A man is rich in proportion to the number of things which he can afford to let alone."

One of the mistakes of our society today is that of living on substitutes. Many people know the price of everything and the value of nothing. They have a false sense of security and a counterfeit feeling of satisfaction. Like a child eating cotton candy at a carnival, these people are enjoying the taste of life but getting nothing substantial to really live on. Then when the storms of life start to blow, they topple over like trees without roots.

The basic problem is this: instead of making *God* the center of their lives, they have made things; instead of worshiping God, they worship things. The Bible has a name for this particular sin—idolatry. A man can bow down to his bankbook and his bonds just as easily as a pagan can bow down to his idols of wood and stone. Our United States coins carry the motto "In God We Trust," but I fear that this motto does not really express our nation's faith. "In Money We Trust" might be a more accurate expression.

Jesus said, "Seek ye first the kingdom of God and his righteousness, and all these things shall be added unto you" (Matt. 6:33). In other words, things—the good things that God wants us to enjoy—are not the center of life, but rather are the extra benefits we receive when God is given His rightful place in our hearts. The man who lives for things and ignores God will lose both, but the man who puts God first will have God and the good things that God wants him to enjoy. This does not mean that every obedient Christian will be rich, but it does mean that he will receive the things God wants him to have in this life. It seems to me that this is a very fair contract. God says to us, "Give Me first place in your life, and I will supply all your needs." David wrote centuries ago, "I have been young and now am old, yet have I not seen the righteous forsaken, nor his seed begging bread" (Ps. 37:25).

When you and I allow Jesus Christ to control our lives, then we gradually discover a whole new set of values. Things that once were so important become very trivial, and things that used to lie on the edges of life suddenly take their rightful place at the very center. We discover that many "things" are just "adult toys," adult pacifiers, to keep us happy until the next novelty comes along. We discover, too, that when Christ is at the center, He gives us a deep satisfaction that nothing else can give. We stop living on substitutes and start enjoying a daily experience of reality.

A rich young man came running up to Jesus one day and sincerely asked how to receive eternal life. He wanted to have his sins forgiven; he wanted to go to heaven. Jesus gave him a strange answer: "Sell all that you have, give it to the poor, and come, follow me." Instead of obeying Christ, the young man turned his back on Him and walked away very unhappy. The reason: he was rich, and he would not give up his riches.

Nobody was ever saved by selling out and giving to the poor. A man is saved by trusting Jesus Christ as his Savior. But this young man trusted his riches, and "no man can serve two masters .... You cannot serve God and money." Jesus told him to give away his money—not that he might be saved, but that he might see the sinfulness of his own heart. His god was money, and it is impossible to trust money and trust Christ at the same time.

I have often thought of what that rich young man missed by living for things. He missed sharing in the victory of Calvary and in the glory of the resurrection. He missed fellowshiping with the risen Christ. He missed praying with the apostles and receiving the Holy Spirit at Pentecost. To be sure, this young man had more of life's riches than all the apostles put together; but they had riches that would last for eternity. Christ was at the center of their lives; and if the center is right, the circumference will take care of itself.

"A man's life does not consist in the abundance of the things that he possesses." Then what does life consist of? Jesus said, "And this is life eternal, that they might know thee, the only true God, and Jesus Christ whom thou hast sent" (John 17:3). Paul said, "For to me to live is Christ" (Phil. 1:21). John wrote, "He that hath the Son, hath life" (I John 5:12). Life is not found in things that fade and decay and lose their value; life is found in a person—in the Person of Jesus Christ.

Jim Eliot, one of the five martyred missionaries, wrote in his diary: "He is no fool to give what he cannot keep, to gain what he cannot lose." We brought nothing into this world, and we will carry nothing out of this world. To live for things is to miss one of the most exciting experiences possible—the day-by-day experience of trusting Christ and making Him the center of our lives . . . the experience of seeing God add to our lives the things that we need just when we need them . . . the experience of claiming God's promises and seeing Him fulfill His Word.

Of what does your life consist? Suppose that tomorrow morning all the things that mean so much to you were taken away? What would you have left? Or suppose you became very ill, and had to lie in a hospital bed for weeks and weeks. In what would you find your joy and satisfaction? Is it possible that you are living on substitutes? If so, then I pity you because, when the substitutes are gone, your life will go with them . . . and you will have nothing worth living for. Why not trust Christ and start living for the true riches—the riches that last for all eternity? Trust Christ and He will give you something worth living for.

23

Getting Out of the Hole

"I waited patiently for the Lord: and he inclined unto me and heard my cry. He brought me up also out of an horrible pit, out of the miry clay, and set my feet upon a rock, and established my goings. And he hath put a new song in my mouth, even praise unto our God" (Ps. 40:1-3).

These words are the personal testimony of a man who had experienced God's power in his life. He knew for himself that the power of God was real and life changing. And he was not ashamed to let everybody know that the Lord had made a difference in his life.

Several dramatic changes took place in his life. The first is this: God lifted him from a pit to a highway. "He brought me up also out of an horrible pit . . . and established my goings."

Frankly, I can't think of a better illustration of the kind of life many people live than that of being trapped in a pit. Many people today are living in pits—living at a level much lower than what God desires for them. In my ministry at the Moody Church in Chicago, I come into contact with all kinds of people; and so many of them are trapped in a pit. They may live in a town house or an exclusive high-rise; but when it comes to the important things of life, they are trapped in a pit.

When I think of a pit, I think of darkness and confinement and monotony. Those words describe the lives of many people today: darkness, confinement, monotony. Walking around the same old pit, covering the same old ground, always on the go but going nowhere. What a monotonous way to live! Yet this is the condition of the person who has never trusted Jesus Christ as Savior. That person is living in a pit, trapped by sin, and unable to get himself out.

But our writer in Psalm 40 says, "He brought me up also out of an horrible pit." You don't have to remain in the pit with its darkness and monotony and confinement. Jesus Christ can lift you up and put your feet on a highway and establish your goings. The Christian is the person who has real freedom. The Christian is the person with a future; he knows where he's going. God establishes the goings of those who trust in Him; He paves the way, He leads the way. Instead of walking around in a pit, we who are saved are walking on the highway that leads to heaven. And, believe me, there is nothing dull or monotonous about the Christian life.

Now, for Jesus to deliver us from that horrible pit of sin meant that He had to descend into the pit Himself. Nobody can escape the pit of sin by using some religious ladder made up of good works and good intentions. No, Jesus Christ had to come down into that horrible pit: on the cross He was made sin for you and me. He came where you are right now. He paid the full penalty for our sins.

The first change was from a pit to a highway. The second change is equally as wonderful: from miry clay to a solid rock. Miry clay is exactly what you would expect to find at the bottom of a pit. You can just picture this man as he walks around the bottom of that pit, sinking deeper and deeper into the clay. Again, this is a picture of the life that is lived without Jesus Christ: a monotonous life of bondage with no real security. For, after all, you can't do much solid building on miry clay.

It's amazing how many people think they have security in this world. They point to their bank accounts, their houses, their investments, their degrees and diplomas, and their jobs. But there is really no security in any of these things. Money can disappear overnight. Investments can fail. Education and training can become obsolete in a short time. Real estate eventually turns to dust. The unsaved man seems to have real security—he seems to have it made; but from God's point of view, he is building on the miry clay.

You remember that Jesus told a story about two builders. One built his house on a rock—he put a foundation under it, and the other man built his house on the shifting sands. Well, both houses were secure—until the storms came. And when the rains came down and the floods came up, the houses faced a crucial test. The house built on the sand was destroyed.

Jesus isn't talking about the construction trade in this story, He's talking about life. He's reminding you and me that we are building our lives, and that we had better have a solid foundation under them. You can't build on the miry clay and expect your life to stand. You have to build on a solid rock.

A few years ago the church I was pastoring embarked on a building program to erect a new auditorium. Before we went too far, we made a series of soil tests; and we discovered that we would be building on an old river bed. Sixty feet down there was shifting sand and miry clay. Of course, you know what we did: we drove in strong supports and laid solid foundations and footings, to make sure the building would stand.

Christ is the rock on which you and I must build our lives. "He brought me up also out of an horrible pit, out of the miry clay, and set my feet upon a rock." Christ is the only sure foundation for life. He is stable, unchanging, never failing. When you trust Him and yield your life to Him, you are building for eternity; and no storms will ever sweep you away.

There is a third change given in Psalm 40: "And he hath

put a new song in my mouth, even praise unto our God." It's the change from a cry to a song of praise.

It takes very little imagination to see and hear this man down in the pit. He walks around in that miry clay, always sinking deeper. And he cries out every once in a while, hoping that somebody will hear. All around me I can hear the tragic cries of people down in the pit. I hear their cries in the music of the day—crying out for somebody to deliver them. I hear their cries as I read the newspaper, as I walk down the busy city streets. We live today in a world that is imprisoned in a pit, crying out for someone to do something.

Now, the Christian doesn't have a cry—he has a song! "And he hath put a new song in my mouth." That's the thrilling thing about being a Christian—God gives you a song and nobody can take it from you. There is no song in sin. There may be foolish songs that people sing in their sins, but the man who doesn't know God has nothing to sing about. When the prodigal son was away from home, living in the far country, he had no song. But when he came home to the father he found a song; and the Bible says, "They began to be merry."

One of the most fascinating verses in the Bible is Mark 14:26: "And when they had sung an hymn, they went out" Can you imagine Jesus Christ facing the agony of the cross, and yet singing a hymn? But He did! He sat at the table with His disciples at that last supper, and He sang a hymn before He went out to die. Because He went through the horror of the cross for us, we have a song to sing. Because He willingly died for us, we have something to sing about.

Does this message find you down in the pit? Are you restless, imprisoned, tired of the monotonous grind of what you think is life? Then trust Jesus Christ and experience the wonderful changes that comes when you yield yourself to Him. He will lift you out of the pit and put you on God's highway. He will take you from the miry clay and put you on a solid rock. And He will exchange that cry of anguish for a song of praise.

24

What You Should Know About God's Will

Every once in a while, a verse from the Bible just jumps out at me and shouts, "Here I am! Listen to me!" Psalm 33:11 is one such verse. "The counsel of the Lord standeth forever, the thoughts of his heart to all generations." There are some encouraging truths in this verse that have been a great help to me on the road to life.

The first truth that jumps out at you from this verse is the fact that *God has a definite plan.* This plan is called "the counsel of the Lord." No matter what circumstances we may be in, no matter how confused the world may seem, God has a plan.

God had a plan when He created the universe. He did not need to consult any engineering firms to get the job done. He simply spoke the Word and a beautiful, orderly universe came into being. "The heavens declare the glory of God, and the firmament showeth his handiwork" (Ps. 19:1). An unprejudiced observer looking at this universe would have to see a Person behind it—a Person with wisdom to plan and power to execute the plan.

God has His counsel for the nations of the world. Napoleon once said, "What is history but a fable agreed upon?" How wrong Napoleon was! A. T. Pierson used to say, "History is His story"—and this is exactly what the Bible teaches. Preaching to the philosophers of Greece, Paul said: "God hath made of one blood all nations of men for to dwell on all the face of the earth, and hath determined the times before appointed, and the bounds of their habitation" (Acts 17:26). The rise and fall of nations is not an accident, it is a divine appointment. The prophet Daniel warned the proud dictator Nebuchadnezzar that "the most High ruleth in the kingdom of men and giveth it to whomsoever he will" (4:25).

If God has a plan for the universe and a plan for the nations, is it not reasonable that He has a plan for our lives individually and personally? Of course He does! When a person trusts Christ as his Savior, he becomes part of a thrilling plan that was ordered from all eternity. I'm not talking about fatalism or the cruel program of a heartless "heavenly dictator." I'm talking about the sovereign will of a loving heavenly Father who wants our lives to glorify Him. God has a divine, loving plan for your life, and the most exciting life possible is a life in the will of God.

There is a second truth from this verse: *God's plan does not change.* It stands forever.

A bit of reflection will show you why God's plan simply cannot change. It's because God does not change. He cannot become better because He is already the sum total of all perfection; and a perfect God could never change for the worse. When God wills a certain thing, it is because this thing is the wisest and best thing possible. God makes no mistakes. "For who hath known the mind of the Lord?" asks Paul in Romans 11:34; "or who hath been his counsellor?" God needs no advice from us, because He knows all things and plans and executes His will in absolute perfection.

Now, the fact that God's counsel stands is a source of great encouragement to me. It means that God's children are not the victims of chance or luck or accidents. No, Romans 8:28 promises, "And we know that all things work together for good to them that love God, to them who are the called according to his purpose." No matter what difficult experiences we may be in right now, God is working out His purpose; and so we don't have to despair or be afraid.

But this truth tells me something else: if God's counsel stands, then those who obey God and seek to fulfill His purposes will also stand forever. This truth was the guiding principle in the life of D. L. Moody. It's expressed in I John 2:17: "He that doeth the will of God abideth forever." When a Christian obeys God, he is on the winning side even though all the world may be pitted against him.

God has a perfect plan, and this plan is not going to change. It stands forever. If we resist God's plan, we don't hurt God's plan—we simply hurt ourselves. But when the child of God obeys the will of God, everything in all the universe works for him.

God has a plan for our lives, and this plan is never going to change. Now for the third fact: *God's plan for your life comes from His heart:* "the thoughts of his heart to all generations." In other words, the will of God is the expression of the love of God.

For some reason, we have the idea that God asks us to do things—or not to do things—because He hates us and wants to make us miserable. Nothing could be further from the truth! When God says no it's because He loves us, just the way a loving parent would say no to a child. And when God says yes it's because He has some wonderful things planned for us, planned for our good and His glory.

A few years ago I was preaching in Canada and a young lady asked me to write something in her autograph book. I signed my name, gave a Bible verse, and then added: "God always gives His best to those who leave the choice with Him."

"Why did you write that?" the girl asked. "Who told you about me?"

I assured her that I knew nothing about her. But it turned out that she was engaged to be married out of the will of God. Well, a few years later, I heard that she had broken her engagement, trained for Christian service, and had met a fine

Christian boy who later became her husband. It was a painful experience for her to break that engagement. But when she yielded to God's loving will, then she really began to live.

You may be questioning God's will, and asking, "Why has this happened? Doesn't God care? Doesn't He love me?" Now, if you are suffering because you have disobeyed God's will, confess it to the Lord and He'll forgive you. But if you know you are in the place of obedience, and you still don't understand—just leave it with the Lord. The will of God comes from the heart of God. He loves us too much to harm us, and He is too wise to make a mistake.

"The counsel of the Lord standeth forever; the thoughts of his heart to all generations."

25

The Living Word

Never underestimate the power of a book. I am told that for every word in Hitler's *Mein Kampf*, 125 people lost their lives in World War II. In 1848, Marx and Engels published a little pamphlet called *The Communist Manifesto*; and today nearly half of the world is living under communist influence. Never underestimate the power of a book, especially the power of God's Book, the Bible. "For the word of God is living and powerful," and the Word of God can change your life.

Nearly fifty years ago, the famous evangelist Gypsy Smith came to Chicago for a series of meetings. A man came to one of the meetings carrying a brick which he intended to throw at the evangelist, so he could start a riot and break up the meeting. When Gypsy Smith walked out to preach, for some reason he looked straight at the young man with the brick, and said: "Young man, Jesus loves you!" And then he began to preach the Word of God.

The next morning, the young man visited Gypsy Smith at the evangelist's hotel room, and told him what he had intended to do. But instead of hitting the preacher with a brick, the young man had been hit by the Word of God. That day he gave his heart to Jesus Christ. Three years later, back in England, Gypsy Smith received a Christmas greeting signed by sixteen students who had just graduated from the Moody Bible Institute. The first name on the list was that of the young man who had carried the brick!

The Word of God has the power to change men's lives. While traveling to a preaching engagement, John Wesley was stopped by a highwayman who took all of his money. As the man started to leave, Wesley said to him: "The time may come when you will regret the course of life in which you are engaged. Remember this: 'The blood of Jesus Christ cleanseth us from all sin'" Years later, when Wesley was leaving a church, a man stopped him and asked him if he remembered being robbed at such a time, in such a place. Wesley said that he did. "I was the man who robbed you," the stranger said. "That single verse was the means of a total change in my life and habits."

Some missionaries to the interior of Brazil stopped to hold a meeting in a village. At the close of the meeting, a young man stepped up and said: "We believe we have a book like yours." He hurried home and came back with a Bible. Ten years before, the man and some friends had been swimming in the river and saw the book caught in some driftwood. The man took it home, dried it out, and started to read it. As a result, twenty villagers became Christians.

"The word of God is living and powerful" (Heb. 4:12). Men may laugh at the Bible, criticize the Bible, and even reject the Bible; but it goes on working in divine power to accomplish God's purposes on this earth. When you and I surrender to the Word of God, then God's power goes to work in our lives and wonderful changes take place. The living Word of God makes us a part of God's eternal plan and releases in our lives God's divine power.

What is the source of the power that is found in the Bible? Why has the Bible weathered all the storms of criticism and opposition that have swept across its pages? What is the secret of its greatness? The answer is really quite simple: the Bible is God's Word. It was not written the way any other book was written, even though human authors were used to pen its pages. It was inspired by the Holy Spirit of God. "All scripture is given by inspiration of God," says II Timothy 3:16; and II Peter 1:21 states, "For the prophecy came not in old time by the will of man, but holy men of God spake as they were moved by the Holy Ghost."

Inspiration is a miracle; so any human definition or explanation that we suggest will have its limitations. But this we know: the Holy Spirit of God used the heads and hearts and hands of holy men of God, and through them wrote the Word of God. Each writer's distinctive personality is retained; yet what he wrote is the very Word of God. It is God's Book, and because it is God's Book, God's power is in it.

Just think for a moment how powerful God's Word really is. There was a time when there was no universe; then God spoke His Word, and worlds came into being. This universe was created by the Word of God, and it is being controlled and held together by that same Word of God.

Or consider the miracles of Jesus Christ. He merely spoke the Word, and diseases vanished from men's bodies; storms quieted down and went to sleep like little babies; men came back to life again! The Word of the Lord is powerful—and this Word is available to you and me today. God still speaks in and through His Word. His promises are just as powerful today as when they were spoken centuries ago. The same Holy Spirit who wrote the Word is with us today to make that Word powerful in our lives. "Heaven and earth shall pass away," said Jesus, "but my words shall not pass away" (Mark 13:31).

As you and I put our faith in the Word of God and obey what God says, we discover that God's power goes to work in our lives. The Spirit of God uses the Word of God to control our minds and hearts, to cleanse us, to create in us desires that glorify God. Living by faith in the Word of God is really the only sensible way to live.

I recall the first time I stepped into a public library, many years ago. Our first grade teacher had marched us all down the boulevard to get our library cards, and from that day on I have been a lover and a reader of good books. I wish now I had kept a record of all the books I have read. But the Bible is radically different from any other book that you and I can read. I can read Shakespeare, or Mark Twain, or Charles Dickens, and enjoy their books without ever having met the authors. But not so with the Bible. The Bible will not really reach your heart unless you know the Author.

You see, the Bible is basically a love story. It tells how men love themselves and love sin, and so have turned away from God's love. And it tells how God in His love has sent His Son, Jesus Christ, to bring men back to God. "For God sent not his Son into the world to condemn the world, but that the world through him might be saved" (John 3:17). This wonderful love story begins in the Garden of Eden, when God shed the blood of an animal in order to clothe the first guilty sinners. It continues at Calvary, where Jesus Christ shed His blood for the sins of the world. And this love story is going to reach its grand conclusion when Jesus Christ returns from heaven to take His people home to live with Him forever.

The Bible has no power in the life of the person who does not personally know the Author. Unless you and I have confessed our need to God and claimed His salvation through faith in Christ, we can never experience the power of the Word of God. "But the natural man [the unsaved man] receiveth not the things of the Spirit of God: for they are foolishness unto him; neither can he know them because they are spiritually discerned" (I Cor. 2:14).

Once you know the Author, the Bible becomes a thrilling new book. I have some books in my library that I thought were pretty dull. Then I met the authors, and I must confess that the books have taken on new interest and meaning. So with the Bible. When you know Jesus Christ personally, then His Word becomes His personal message to you . . . and this message releases God's power in your life.

Spend time daily with the Word of God. Read it carefully.

Pray over it. Meditate on it. Memorize it and think about it during the day. Claim the promises that God gives you, and be sure to obey the commandments as well. Then you will know what it means when the Bible says, "For the word of God is living and powerful."

26

God's Answer for Discouragement

This poem was written by a man planning to commit suicide.

> To whom can I speak today?
>> The gentle man has perished,
>> The violent man has access to everybody.
> To whom can I speak today?
>> The iniquity that smites the land,
>> It has no end.
> To whom can I speak today?
>> There are no righteous men,
>> The earth is surrendered to criminals.

The interesting thing is this: the poem was not written by a frustrated twentieth century businessman. It was written by an Egyptian citizen over four thousand years ago. Violence and crime and corruption and thoughts of suicide are not modern problems, are they? They are ancient problems—and they have an ancient solution.

It takes little imagination to understand the mind of our anonymous Egyptian poet. He saw crime and violence all around him. The old values were changing. The good man was hanging on the scaffold and the evil man was sitting on the throne. There seemed to be no justice, no hope, no future. After pondering the situation, he decided that there was only one way out—to commit suicide.

Of course, suicide did not solve any problems. It never does. But here was a man who had absolutely no resources to depend on, no one to turn to in his hour of need. "To whom can I speak today?" he asks, and never does get an answer. It's the picture of a lonely, helpless man at the crossroads of life, with no one to help him.

I'm sure that this picture can be multiplied many times today. All around us are frustrated people who simply don't know what to do. Their world is collapsing around them. Everything they used to depend on has been destroyed; their foundations are gone. They don't know where to turn, and perhaps they may be entertaining thoughts of ending it all.

It might interest you to know that some of the greatest men in the Bible had their hours of disappointment and defeat, and some of them even asked God to take their lives. I'm not saying they were right; but I am saying that they went through experiences that were terribly disillusioning, and yet they came out victoriously.

For example, the great Jewish leader Moses became so discouraged one day that he asked God to kill him. Listen to the record from Numbers 11: "Then Moses heard the people weep throughout their families . . . and Moses also was displeased. And Moses said unto the Lord, Wherefore hast thou afflicted thy servant? . . . Have I conceived all this people? Have I begotten them? . . . I am not able to bear all this people alone, because it is too heavy for me. And if thou deal thus with me, kill me . . . and let me not see my wretchedness."

Moses was discouraged because he was carrying a heavy burden and the people did not appreciate his leadership. Where would the nation of Israel have been without the leadership of Moses? How often it is that those who do the most for us are the least appreciated. When Moses heard the people weeping and complaining, his heart sank within him.

Listen to the great prophet Elijah as he sits under the juniper tree: "It is enough; now, O Lord, take away my life; for I am not better than my fathers."

Elijah was discouraged because he felt he was a failure. He had met the false prophets face to face and had defeated them; yet the people had not rallied to Elijah's side in the great revival that he had longed to see. When Queen Jezebel threatened to kill him, Elijah fled for his life. And then he asked God to kill him! If Elijah had really wanted to die, he should have surrendered to Jezebel. How often we say and do foolish things simply because we are discouraged.

Suppose God would have answered the prayers of these men and taken their lives? Think of all they would have missed. Moses would have missed seeing God's wonders in the wilderness. He would have missed that great farewell at Jordan, recorded in the Book of Deuteronomy. He would have missed commissioning Joshua to take his place. And he would have missed seeing the beautiful Land of Promise.

Elijah would have missed his fellowship with young Elisha; he would have missed the joy of training the new prophet to take his place. And he would have missed a glorious chariot ride into heaven! Yes, it's a good thing God does not answer our prayers when we are discouraged and defeated. If He did, we would miss so many blessings.

Our Egyptian poet had no one to speak to. "To whom can I speak today?" was his question. But Moses and Elijah had someone to speak to: they took their disappointments to the Lord. We may not agree with their prayers, but we do agree with their praying.

> Have we trials and temptations?
> Is there trouble anywhere?
> We should never be discouraged;
> Take it to the Lord in prayer.

That's the first secret of victory over discouragement: take it to the Lord in prayer. Open your heart; tell Him just the way you feel. The psalmist David puts it this way in Psalm 142: "I cried unto the Lord with my voice . . . I poured out my complaint before him; I showed before him my trouble. When my spirit was overwhelmed within me, then thou knewest my path. . . . Attend unto my cry, for I am brought very low. Bring my soul out of prison, that I may praise thy name."

When life seems the darkest, then God's dawn is about to break. He sees the end from the beginning, and He has a perfect plan for your life. "For I know the plans I have for you," the Lord says in Jeremiah 29:11, "plans for welfare and not for calamity, to give you a future and a hope." Disappointment is often "His appointment." And God permits these difficulties to come our way, not to discourage us, but to encourage us to look away from changing circumstances to the unchanging God who is on the throne.

Even the great apostle Paul had his days of discouragement when it seemed he would have to give up. This is what he writes: "For we would not, brethren, have you ignorant of our trouble which came to us in Asia, that we were pressed out of measure, above strength, insomuch that we despaired even of life. But we had the sentence of death in ourselves, that we should not trust in ourselves, but in God which raiseth the dead; who delivered us from so great a death, and doth deliver; in whom we trust that he will yet deliver us" (II Cor. 1:8-10).

The answer to discouragement is not to run away, but to run to God. "God is our refuge and strength, a very present help in trouble" (Ps. 46:1). That word *trouble* means "tight places"—"a very present help in tight places." Moses prayed, and God met his need; Elijah prayed, and God met his need. And if you and I will pray, God will meet our needs as well.

Now, when we pray, God does not always change the circumstances around us. But He does put new strength and hope within us so that we can face the circumstances courageously and keep on going. It has often been said that what life does *to* us depends on what life finds *in* us. If we are filled with defeat and despair, then life will crush us. If we are filled with faith and with God's power, then life can never overcome us. Instead of being victims, we will be victors; for, "If God be for us, who can be against us?" (Rom. 8:31).

When you are discouraged, follow this counsel from the Word of God. First, don't do anything drastic. Never, *never* make an important decision when you are going through the black night of despair. Second, turn to God and tell Him just the way you feel. Open your heart, as David did, and "pour out your complaint before him." Third, wait on the Lord. He has His purposes and He has His times. To run ahead of Him would mean to miss the wonderful things He has planned for you. Finally, rest on His promises. Spend much time with your Bible, and claim the promises of the Word. When the night is the darkest we see the stars the clearest; and when life is dark, the promises of God shine like stars.

If you are one of God's children, and if you are seeking to do His will, you can be sure that, in spite of circumstances, "all things are working together for good" (Rom. 8:28). One day soon the light will dawn, the shadows will flee away, and you will understand why God permitted you to suffer as you did. But until that day, "Commit thy way unto the Lord, trust also in him, and he shall bring it to pass" (Ps. 37:5).

27

Give Me Liberty

On July 4, 1776, the Second Continental Congress declared the thirteen American colonies free and independent from Great Britain. The Declaration of Independence is the only major national document of the United States that actually mentions the name of God. He is called "Nature's God," "The Creator," and "The Supreme Judge of the World." The fathers of our American freedom recognized that God's hand was at work in the affairs of the new nation. But far more important than the political liberty that we enjoy is the spiritual liberty we have in Christ. Jesus said, "And ye shall know the truth, and the truth shall make you free" (John 8:32).

Jesus spoke these words to some Jewish leaders who were arguing with Him. "We have never been in bondage to any man!" they said. "Why do you talk to us about freedom?" But even while Jesus was teaching them, the nation of Israel was under the authority of Rome. Palestine was a police state, there were Roman soldiers everywhere, and Roman officials were busy collecting tolls and taxes.

The masses of people wanted Jesus to set them free from

Roman tyranny, but not from sin. After Jesus fed the five thousand, the people wanted to make Him their king. In fact, even the disciples had the idea that Jesus would go to Jerusalem, defeat Rome, and establish the Jewish kingdom. The people wanted political liberty, but were ignorant of their deepest need—spiritual liberty. Even after Christ rose from the dead, some of His followers were still looking for a political revolution. The two men on the road to Emmaus said, "But we trusted that it had been he which should have set Israel free."

Certainly political bondage is terrible, and we ought to pray for the people in our world who don't enjoy the liberties that many of us enjoy. But of what value is political liberty if a man is in bondage to sin? That's the kind of bondage Jesus was talking about when He said, "And ye shall know the truth, and the truth shall make you free." He saw the people enslaved by sin, and even enslaved by a religious system that gave them no joy or peace.

Jesus Christ came to this earth to give men spiritual liberty, to set men free from fear and selfishness and sin. The chains of sin are forged slowly and silently, while men think they are living in liberty. The prodigal son in the far country enjoyed his freedom away from home; yet all the while he was putting himself into bondage. This is one of the deceitful things about sin: it promises freedom but always leads to slavery. And the chains of sin cannot be broken in our own strength. It takes one stronger than we are to set us free, and that person is Jesus Christ. The battle in the world today is between truth and lies. Jesus said, "I am the truth." He also said, "The devil is a liar." Satan enslaves men with his lies, but Christ sets them free with His truth.

This battle began back at the beginning of human history. Satan came to Eve in the garden and asked her a question: "Yea, hath God said . . .?" He questioned the word of God. Then Satan told a lie: "God knows that if you eat of the tree, you will be like God." Eve believed Satan's lie, disobeyed the Lord, and sinned. Then she led Adam into sin. Because they believed Satan's lie, they put themselves into bondage. And from that day to this, mankind has been enslaved by sin.

Jesus Christ came to set us free, and His weapon is truth. "And ye shall know the truth, and the truth shall make you free." What is this truth? Well, for one thing, it is the truth about ourselves. We can never be set free until we admit that we are enslaved. It's rather interesting that our modern psychologists believe this same principle. They try to get the patient to face reality, no matter how painful this may be, because it is only after we have faced the truth about ourselves that we can be changed.

For several years, I worked with a friend in helping alcoholics. We visited homes together and spent hours trying to help men find liberty in Christ. When I first began this ministry, I was shocked at the way my friend talked to the alcoholics. He was honest—blunt—sometimes he seemed even cruel! He saw my reactions to his methods, and said to me: "Preacher, I used to be an alcoholic. I know what it's like. Somebody had to shock me into seeing myself like I really was, before the Lord could do anything for me."

Have you faced the truth about yourself? When you look at yourself in the mirror, do you give yourself the correct name—deceiver, cheat, boaster, fearful, selfish—whatever your real name may be? This is the first step toward true liberty: admitting the truth about ourselves. And, after all, there's no reason to hide, because God knows what we are already.

Step two is facing the truth about Christ: He is the redeemer, the only one who can set us free from sin. Religion alone can never do it. In fact, religion can put a man into greater bondage, as he tries to live up to a standard he can never reach in his own power. Reformation alone will never do it. Merely changing our habits can never change our hearts. No, the only answer is what the Bible calls "redemption."

Many cities in our nation have places called a "redemption center." This is where the busy housewives go to turn in their trading stamps and pick up valuable merchandise. Calvary is God's redemption center. It is at the cross that we give Christ our sins and He gives us freedom. He was bound like a criminal and crucified like the lowest murderer, in order that He might set us free. Redemption demands a price, and the only price God will accept is the blood of Jesus Christ. The choirs in heaven sing, "Thou art worthy . . . for thou wast slain and hast redeemed us to God by thy blood."

At this point, someone may be saying, "You preachers are always talking about blood! Doesn't Jesus save us by His example or His teaching?" No, He doesn't. He saves us and sets us free by His death and resurrection. After all, wasn't our political freedom purchased with blood? When Sir Winston Churchill spoke to the British people that dark day in May 1940, he said, "I have nothing to offer but blood, toil, tears, and sweat"—and the free world applauded him. Back in 1787, when Thomas Jefferson wrote: "The tree of liberty must be refreshed from time to time with the blood of patriots and tyrants," nobody was offended. Then, why be offended when Jesus tells us that blood must be shed if men are to be set free from sin?

"The truth shall make you free"—first, the truth about yourself, and then, the truth about Jesus Christ . . . that Christ died for your sins. He can set you free if you will but trust Him. Christ did not die as a martyr; He died as a liberator. He defeated every enemy—Satan, sin, death, and hell—and He alone is the mighty conqueror.

Once you believe God's truth and trust God's Son, you begin a new kind of life—a life lived in truth and love, not lies and hatred. When a person lives by lies, he must always be fighting a battle, covering up, pretending. But when he lives by God's truth, he experiences a wonderful liberty and joy and openness. He no longer has to pretend. He knows the truth about himself, he knows that God knows what he is like, and he knows that God has accepted Him and forgiven him. This is the thrilling liberty that we have in Jesus Christ.

28

Steadfastness

The Gospel of Luke has always been my favorite Gospel. I appreciate Matthew's picture of the King, and Mark's record of Jesus the Servant, and John's majestic story of the eternal Son of God. But my heart finds its home in the Gospel of Luke. I'll tell you why: it is especially the Gospel of sympathy and compassion. In it we meet individual people, not crowds. We meet Jesus the great physician as He tenderly meets the needs of all kinds of people. Luke is the Gospel of compassion and sympathy, of childhood and the home, of singing and weeping. Luke is the story of a journey Jesus made, a journey to the cross. Luke says about Jesus, "He steadfastly set his face to go to Jerusalem" (9:51). Nearly half of the Gospel of Luke is devoted to the record of Jesus' last journey to Jerusalem. He knew why He was going there: He was going there to die.

When Jesus first told His disciples about this trip to Jerusalem, they simply couldn't believe it. In fact, Peter took Jesus to one side and rebuked Him. "Pity yourself, Lord," Peter said. "This should never happen to you!" But it *was* true: He was going to Jerusalem, not to be crowned, but to be crucified.

You see, from the very beginning, Jesus was controlled by a master purpose. At the age of twelve, He said to Mary and Joseph when they found Him in the temple, "Don't you know that I must be about my Father's business?" When Jesus came down to the Jordan River to be baptized and to begin His ministry, John the Baptist cried, "Behold, the Lamb of God which taketh away the sin of the world." Jesus Himself said to Nicodemus, "As Moses lifted up the serpent in the wilderness, even so must the Son of man be lifted up." He was speaking, of course, about the cross.

So when Jesus set out to make that last journey to Jerusalem, it was not as a traveler seeing the sights of the holy city, or as a spectator at a religious festival. No, He made that last journey as God's sacrifice for sins. He was going to Jerusalem to die for you and for me, and for the sins of the whole world.

The more I think about it, the more wonderful this journey becomes. As you walk with Jesus through the pages of Luke's Gospel, you find Him thinking about others, not about Himself. If you knew that you were going to die a cruel death on a Roman cross, would you be thinking about others? I'm afraid most of us would be thinking about ourselves and perhaps feeling sorry for ourselves. But not Jesus. As He makes that last journey to Jerusalem, He pauses to teach the people, to preach the gospel, to heal the sick, to give new life and new hope to sinners.

This is the message Luke is trying to get across to us: Jesus is the friend of those in need, and He is never too busy to stop and listen to our problems, and help us bear life's burdens. Jesus Christ hasn't changed: He is the same yesterday, and today, and forever. He is never far away, He is never too busy, He is never indifferent or unconcerned. He knows about your needs and He is able to help you.

"Jesus steadfastly set his face to go to Jerusalem." This was not an easy journey for Him to make. You see, for the most part, He had to make it alone. True, He had His disciples with Him; but they really didn't understand what was happening. They were quite sure He was making a mistake when He told them He would be rejected and cruci-fied. In spite of the fact that Jesus was facing Jerusalem alone, He steadfastly set His face and kept right on going.

This encourages me. There are times in all of our lives when God calls us to make a journey—to do a special job—and others may not understand what it is all about. We have to walk alone. And how easy it is to quit. How easy it is to argue with ourselves and turn away from the goal to take a more comfortable detour. Jesus didn't do that: He stead-fastly set His face to go to Jerusalem, and nothing turned Him away. He was able to say to His Father, "I have finished the work that you gave me to do."

Perhaps you are facing a difficult task. Your Jerusalem is before you—your Gethsemane, your Calvary. And perhaps you are saying to yourself, "I just can't do it. The journey is too much for me." My friend, get your eyes off yourself and off the road that lies before you, and fix your eyes on Jesus Christ. Do you see Him making His way toward Jerusalem, knowing what lies before Him? Can you see Him lifting His eyes toward heaven and saying to His Father, "Not my will but Thine be done"? Jesus made His journey successfully, and He can help you finish your journey and accomplish God's will.

It is always too soon to quit. The journey of life is not an easy one; it wasn't easy for Jesus. But as children of God, we can draw on Christ's power and make that journey victorious-ly. I recall standing in Westminster Abbey at the spot where David Livingstone is buried, and something that Livingstone said came back to me. "Do you know what it was that sustained me in the African bush?" Livingstone asked a congregation when he returned to England. "Do you know what it was that kept me going? It was the promise of Jesus Christ—'Lo, I am with you always.' "

That promise that kept Livingstone going can keep you and me going, too—"Lo, I am with you always." In fact, this promise sustained Jesus Christ as He walked toward the cross. He said to His disciples, "All of you will forsake me, but the Father is with me. He will not leave me alone."

Jesus was going to the hardest *place* possible, to endure the hardest *test* possible: death on the cross. Have you ever noticed that Jesus never avoided the hard places of life? From the very beginning of His earthly life, He was found in the hard place. He was born in a stable. He lived in a poor carpenter's home. "Foxes have dens, and birds have nests, but the Son of man has nowhere to lay his head." Jesus never looked for shortcuts or easy detours. He walked the road to Jerusalem and deliberately chose the difficult way.

You and I need to follow His example. How easy it is for us to accept the easiest jobs, carry the lightest burdens, walk the most comfortable roads. What God needs today are men and women who will steadfastly set their faces and tackle the difficult jobs and get them done. I fear that some of us are a bit too comfortable in our faith. We carry enough Christian responsibility to maintain some kind of respectable testimony, but we cannot really say that our road is a Calvary road. Our cross is stuck on the lapel or hanging from a gold chain around the neck; it isn't on our back. We can't honestly say that it costs us anything to be a Christian.

Perhaps you are thinking of giving up your Christian service because the journey has become too difficult. That Sunday school class is so hard to teach, or it's costing so much to go visiting or to hold that office in your church. Many a pastor is discouraged and seriously thinking of quitting and finding an easier place. I would urge you to steadfastly set your face the way Jesus did, and keep on doing the job. Every life has its Jerusalem road, its Gethsemane, its Calvary. And, thank God, every life has its Easter day of resurrection joy and victory! Christ first had to suffer, and then enter into His glory; and you and I are not going to alter God's methods.

Moses was ready to quit, but the Lord gave him new strength, and he steadfastly set his face and accomplished God's will. David felt like giving up, but instead he trusted God and set his face like a flint to finish the work God gave him to do. Even the great apostle Paul came to a place in his life where it seemed impossible to go on. He was pressed out

133

of measure, above strength, ready to die. But he put his faith in God and steadfastly set his face to walk the road God had marked out for him. The secret, my friend, is faith. Yield yourself to Christ, draw upon His power and patience, and steadfastly set your face to go to your Jerusalem. You will discover that God will see you through, and that at the end of the road is the glory of God.

29

Courage to Live

A soldier was home on furlough before being sent to the front lines. He visited his grandfather who was an invalid, afflicted with a painful disease. Both the grandfather and the grandson were Christians; so they had a good time discussing spiritual matters. As he prepared to leave, the boy said to his grandfather, "Grandpa, pray for me that I'll have the courage to die." The old man looked up through eyes that revealed the pain he was enduring, and he said, "I will, my son; and please pray for me that I'll have the courage to live."

Certainly it takes courage to die, but sometimes it takes more courage to live. When a Christian dies, he goes to be with Christ, which is far better. But to live day after day, year after year, with pain or difficult circumstances is quite something else. Perhaps this is why more than twenty thousand persons a year commit suicide in our country, and many thousands more make the attempt but fail. I understand that suicide ranks tenth as a cause of death in the United States, and that it is becoming more and more prevalent among college students and teen-agers.

Quite frankly, suicide doesn't solve any problems, no

matter how noble men might try to make suicide appear. I'm sure that in many cases the person has a mental or emotional disturbance and perhaps is not totally responsible for his decision. But more than one person with a clear mind has contemplated taking his own life, simply because life had become too difficult for him.

Moses had this experience, and Moses was a man of God. One day he was so overwhelmed by the problems of the nation of Israel that he said to God, "I am not able to bear all this people alone, because it is too heavy for me. And if thou deal thus with me, kill me I pray thee . . . and let me not see my wretchedness" (Num. 11:14-15). Of course, God knew that His servant was overwrought and discouraged; and God did not answer his foolish prayer. The prophet Elijah became discouraged and also prayed that God would take his life. So the pressures of life are real, and it takes courage to face life.

This is where Jesus Christ comes in. He died to give us life—eternal life; and He lives today to help us face life and live it victoriously. Being a Christian means more than going to heaven someday, as wonderful as that is. Being a Christian means having the courage to face life today, and face it as a victor and not a victim. It means keeping on when others are quitting. It means singing a song when others are complaining. It means joining the apostle Paul in that great affirmation of faith: "I can do all things through Christ who strengthens me" (Phil. 4:13).

Have you ever thought of the difficulties that Jesus faced when He was living here on earth? He knew the meaning of poverty because He was born into the home of a poor carpenter. He grew up in the despised village of Nazareth. It is likely that while He was just a lad, His foster father Joseph died, leaving Mary a widow. There were other brothers and sisters in the home; so it must have been a crowded, uncomfortable situation. Jesus knew what it was to work with His hands and earn a living. He went through the difficulties of life that you and I go through, and yet He never became discouraged.

When Jesus started His public ministry, He knew what it

was to be laughed at and misunderstood. Some of His friends and relatives even said He was crazy. They called Him a glutton and a drunkard; they said He was demon possessed. He was misunderstood even by those who should have best understood. His life was threatened. When He displayed love, men retaliated with hatred. When He spoke the truth, they spoke lies. Believe me, Christ's life here on earth was not an easy one.

And think of the humiliating way that He died. He was arrested illegally. The witnesses lied about Him. The soldiers, instead of protecting Him and giving Him His rights, persecuted Him and laughed at Him. They spat in His face—they struck Him with their hands—they crowned Him with thorns—and then they crucified Him. And through all of this inhuman treatment, Jesus was able to say: "Father, forgive them for they know not what they do."

Now my point is this: Jesus Christ went through every trial and testing that you can ever go through—and He won the victory. If His crucifixion looked like a defeat, His resurrection from the dead changed all that. We look back at the cross and realize that it was not a defeat but a tremendous victory. On the cross Jesus conquered sin and death and hell. Every enemy bows at His feet.

That is why Paul could write in Philippians 4:13, "I can do all things through Christ who strengthens me." Paul faced far more difficulties in life than you and I face; yet he came through in victory. Why? Because of anything he had in himself? No! It was because he permitted Christ to work in and through his life. Paul's testimony was, "Not I, but Christ liveth in me" (Gal. 2:20). The Christian life is not imitation, it is incarnation: Christ living His life in and through us. This is what gives us the courage to live.

Have you ever tried to put together a picture puzzle without first having seen the picture? It can be done, but it's very difficult. Once you have seen the picture, you know where the various colors belong. Well, life is something like this. Because today we cannot see the total picture, we don't know exactly where the individual pieces belong; and we get discouraged. We think God has forgotten us, or worse yet, that He has turned against us. It is then that we lose the courage to live, and life becomes a monotonous grind instead of an exciting experience.

Let's lay hold of a basic fact: God sees the total picture. It really isn't necessary for me to know the end from the beginning, because God already knows. God does not have to give us reasons, because He gives us promises. We say, "Oh, if I only knew what tomorrow holds, I'd be happier." My friend, if you and I knew what tomorrow holds, we might be terribly frightened. The important thing is not to worry about tomorrow, but to live for Christ today.

Life has never been easy. This world is a battleground, not a playground. Jesus said, "In the world you shall have tribulation, but be of good cheer, I have overcome the world." The difficulties of life are God's tools for building character and making us more like Jesus Christ. I'm sure that all of us have times of depression when we feel like throwing in the towel and quitting, but those are the times we need to turn to Christ and let His power go to work.

Yes, it takes courage to live and it takes courage to die. In ourselves, we don't have this courage. But through faith in Christ we can face life with confidence and know that He will see us through. He never leaves us; He never forsakes us. His power is always available for every demand of life. He can give us what we need—patience, wisdom, kindness, love, understanding, moral courage. He never fails.

I don't know your special problems right now. Perhaps you have come to the end of your rope and you're ready to give up. Please listen once again to the promise of God, spoken through the apostle Paul: "I can do all things through Christ who strengthens me." Invite Jesus Christ into your life. Take that step of faith. He died for you, He is alive today, and He can move right into your life and make you what God wants you to be. Surrender to His will; don't try to work things out your own way. Follow His plan, trust His power, and Christ will see you through.

30

Start Really Living

Years ago the American poet Edgar A. Guest wrote these words:

> I have to live with myself, and so
> I want to be fit for myself to know. . . .

Living with others can be a problem, but sometimes living with ourselves may be a greater problem. In fact, if we cannot live with ourselves, it's doubtful whether others can live with us, either. What is the secret of getting along with yourself? Do you have to live with regrets and self-condemnation? Of course not. Your faith in Jesus Christ can make you into the kind of person you really want to live with.

Why is it that some people have a hard time living with themselves? Let me suggest some reasons. One common cause is *regret*. Often people will say to me, "It worries me that I wasn't kinder to my brother before he died." Or, "As I look back, I can see that I didn't treat my employer as I should; and this upsets me." Regret—the ghosts of the past that haunt us—can make it difficult for us to live with ourselves.

And, of course, there is always the problem of *sin*. David cried out in Psalm 51, "My sin is ever before me!" How many people have dark pages in their diary; and when these pages flash into their minds, they hate themselves.

Some people can't live with themselves because of *wasted or misused opportunities.*

> For of all sad words of tongue or pen,
> The saddest are these, "It might have been!"

And multitudes of people are making life miserable for themselves and others by repeating, "If only—if only!" They dream of a life that can never be, because of lost opportunity.

Failure is another thing that makes it difficult for us to live with ourselves. Years ago, in some cultures, the man who failed was expected to commit suicide to atone for his failure. Today most people don't kill themselves; they spend the rest of their lives torturing themselves, punishing themselves for mistakes they have made. We live in a world that demands success. Success is the measure of a man's worth, according to most people. Let a man fail and he must live with that burden for the rest of his life.

I don't know what it is that may be robbing you of your personal peace and satisfaction. There may be something in your life right now that is making it difficult for you to live with yourself. Perhaps it is regret—you feel you have wronged a loved one, or that you didn't do what you were supposed to do. Perhaps it is sin, and the past is haunting you. Perhaps you are weeping over lost opportunities, and you are wondering how different life would have been if only—if only. Maybe you have failed somewhere along the line, and that failure stabs you in the heart every time you think of it.

I have good news for you: Jesus Christ knows all about these problems and wants to solve them for you. He knows your regrets, your sins, your wasted opportunities, your failures—and He loves you just the same. He wants to liberate you from this bondage that is robbing you of peace and joy. Jesus said, "If the Son therefore shall make you free, ye shall be free indeed" (John 8:36).

People who find it difficult to love themselves usually have one thing in common: they are haunted by something from

140

their past. The past has a way of moving into the present and making the future look very dark. Someone has said that most people today are being crucified between two thieves: the regrets of yesterday and the fears of tomorrow; and this keeps them from enjoying the blessings of today.

Now, this is where Jesus Christ, our Savior, steps into the problem and starts to solve it for us. You see, when you turn yourself over to Him, He completely washes away your past—every sin, every mistake, every foolish act. In fact, He promises to forget our past and never hold it against us. "Their sins and their iniquities will I remember no more." (Heb. 10:17). The trouble with us is that we remember what God forgets—and then we forget what God wants us to remember! There's no reason why you and I should sit and brood over our shameful past. Christ died for our sins. The blood of Jesus Christ washes away our sins. The old record has been destroyed, and we have made a new beginning in Christ.

If any man had reason to regret his past, it was the apostle Paul. Think of it—a proud Pharisee, a persecutor of good men, and even a murderer! Paul didn't try to bury his past or whitewash it. No, he did something better: he turned it over to Jesus Christ and asked Christ to use his past for God's glory. Read Paul's letters and notice that whenever he talks about his past, he always connects it with the grace of God. "Before I was saved," Paul writes to Timothy, "I was a blasphemer, and a persecutor, and injurious . . . and the grace of our Lord was exceeding abundant with faith and love which is in Christ Jesus" (I Tim. 1:12-14). Paul didn't shackle himself to the past; he let God take his past and make a wonderful future out of it.

Think of the apostle Peter, the man who openly denied the Lord Jesus three times. When Peter wept over his sins, Christ forgave him; and Peter didn't allow his past mistakes to hinder his present ministry. Why, just a few weeks after he had denied the Lord, Peter faced the nation of Israel and dared to say, "But ye denied the Holy One and the Just!" Peter knew that his sins were held against him no more.

That's the first step in learning to live with yourself: turn your past over to Christ and accept by faith His promise of forgiveness. In Christ we are new creations; old things have passed away and no longer have power over us. "If we confess our sins," promises I John 1:9, "he is faithful and just to forgive us our sins, and to cleanse us from all unrighteousness."

People who can't live with themselves often have a hard time accepting themselves. They wish they were somebody else. Why was I born plain instead of beautiful? Why am I ordinary instead of talented? Why do the breaks never come my way? You really cannot live with yourself unless you accept yourself, and this means accepting yourself with all your weaknesses and faults and failures. Believe me, we all have them! The fact that you are a child of God, going to heaven, doesn't exclude you from the burdens and disappointments of life. It does mean, however, that these disappointments don't have to chain you and rob you of your happiness in Christ.

Once you realize that God has accepted you—and He knows more about you than you know about yourself—then it becomes easier for you to accept yourself. God loves you—God knows your inner struggles—He sees the end from the beginning—but in Christ He has accepted you. You are important to Him. He has put His very life within you. But remember, you have this treasure in an earthen vessel, a frail body of clay; and the road from here to heaven is not going to be easy.

It's wonderful the way God weaves the fabric of our lives. From our earthbound viewpoint, the pattern doesn't really make sense, because we're looking at the wrong side of the fabric. One of these days, God will turn things around and we'll see the total pattern; then we'll understand why things happened as they did. What we today consider to be a serious blunder may turn out to be a great victory when the light of eternity shines on it. And that service we performed that we're so ashamed of today might win the greatest reward from Jesus Christ. And the very people we feel we wronged may throw their arms around us and thank us for the help we gave them. God is still working all things together for our good and His glory; so trust Him to paint life's picture the way He wants it to be, and reserve your judgment until that day when He opens our eyes and we see life as it truly is.

One more thought in closing. You remember that King David wanted to build a temple to the glory of God, but God would not allow him. But God did say to David, "Whereas it was in thine heart to build a house unto my name, thou didst well that it was in thine heart" (I Kings 8:18). God knows the desires of your heart—desires that perhaps cannot be fulfilled because the opportunities are past. But He sees your heart, and He will reward you for what He sees in your heart. Don't fill your heart with vain regrets or self-condemnation. Open your heart to the love of Christ, tell Him what is in your heart, and He will meet your need. After all, Jesus came to heal the brokenhearted and to set the captives free. He forgives the past, He accepts you as you are and loves you, and He can use even the disappointments of life to glorify His name.

Notes

Dr. Warren W. Wiersbe is heard on "Songs in the Night," the international radio voice of the Moody Church of Chicago. It is a once-weekly, half-hour radio program featuring a unique format of inspirational thoughts by Dr. Wiersbe, interspersed with a variety of sacred music. Continuity is provided throughout the entire broadcast by the smooth resonance of the mighty four-manual, 4400-pipe, 73-rank Reuter organ of the church.

Started in the spring of 1943 by Torrey Johnson, then pastor of the Midwest Bible Church in Chicago, "Songs in the Night" achieved early fame less than a year later when it moved to The Village Church in suburban Western Springs, Illinois. It was there that the pastor, Billy Graham, first teamed together with soloist George Beverly Shea for the purpose of the "Songs in the Night" broadcast. In succeeding years, Peter Stam, III, and Lloyd Fesmire pastored the church and ministered as radio speakers.

Then in 1968 "Songs in the Night" moved its base of operations to Chicago's historic Moody Church through the efforts of Dr. George Sweeting, who was then pastor. Dr. Wiersbe joined the program in January, 1972, after Dr. Sweeting moved on to the presidency of the Moody Bible Institute.

Today, with thirty years of continuous broadcasting behind it, "Songs in the Night" ministers on more than two hundred stations each week, including thirteen foreign outlets. Domestically, nearly half the stations air the program in stereo. God has singularly honored this program which brings untold blessings and comfort to millions of listeners each week. This book contains thirty of the messages which Dr. Wiersbe presented on "Songs in the Night" during his first year with the program.

Donald H. Smith